THE DRUMS
WOULD ROLL

Overleaf: An unidentified cavalry bandsman from Fort
Riley holds his dress helmet with the lyre overlay device.
He is a picture-perfect example of the regulation uniform,
with the exception of the additional gold cord suspended
below his neck for extra ornamentation. (Joseph J. Pennell
Collection, Kansas Collection, University of Kansas Libraries)

THE DRUMS WOULD ROLL

A PICTORIAL HISTORY OF
US ARMY BANDS ON THE AMERICAN FRONTIER 1866–1900

THOMAS C. RAILSBACK & JOHN P. LANGELLIER

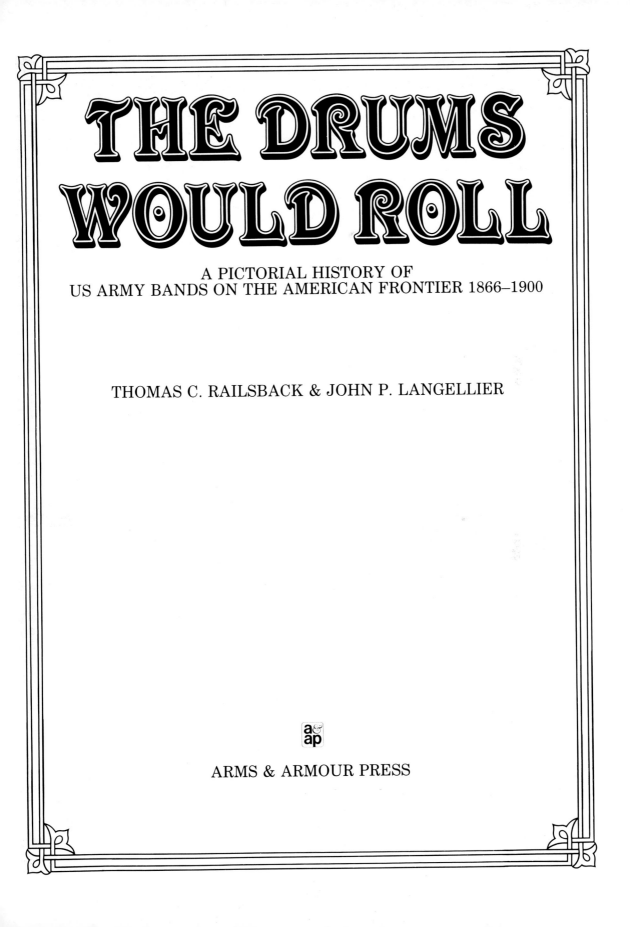

ARMS & ARMOUR PRESS

First published in Great Britain in 1987 by Arms and
Armour Press Ltd., Link House, West Street, Poole,
Dorset BH15 1LL.

Distributed in the USA
by Sterling Publishing Co. Inc.,
2 Park Avenue, New York, NY 10016.

Distributed in Australia
by Capricorn Link (Australia) Pty. Ltd.,
P.O. Box 665, Lane Cove, New South Wales 2066.

British Library Cataloguing in Publication data:
Railsback, Thomas C.
The drums would roll: a pictorial history
of US Army Bands on the American Frontier
1866–1900 – (Old Army Series; 1)
1. Bands (Music) – United States
2. Military music – United States – History
and criticism
I. Title   II. Langellier, John P.   III. Series
785'.06'71   ML1311

ISBN 0-85368-876-1

Edited and designed by Roger Chesneau; typeset by
Typesetters (Birmingham) Ltd.; printed and bound
in Italy in association with Keats European
Production Ltd., London.

CONTENTS

'Oh, the Drums would roll upon my soul, This is the style we'd go
Forty miles a day on beans and hay, In the Regular Army O! . . .'

The Regular Army O!, Edward Harrigan

To Dr. Leo Oliva, Dr. Don Rickey
and Professor Lyle Dilley,
in appreciation for everything they did
to make this publication possible.

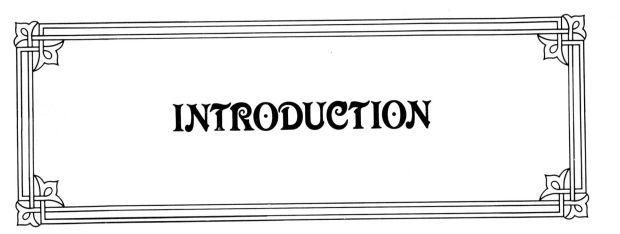

INTRODUCTION

The commander's wife and daughter would arrive soon from the East. This news spread throughout Arizona Territory and was cause for celebration. There would be a fine dress ball to welcome the two women. In preparation, 'the band of the infantry was daily practicing the latest and most attractive music, imported from New York expressly for the occasion, and their energetic and eccentric leader was grinning and capering and writhing himself into the verge of convulsions in his efforts to throw *espressione* into the waltz' he had composed for the Colonel's ladies. Indeed, the bandmaster 'was always composing and dedicating waltzes to the ladies of the senior officers.'[1]

Although this description of western military life came from a work of fiction by Captain Charles King, the passage faithfully captured a typical episode at many United States Army installations during the era following the Civil War.[2] The bands played an important part in the social life of several posts in the West. They offered concerts and provided the orchestra for dances and even opera. Some events were quite elaborate. King remarked that 'never did the "swellest" German at Delmonico's present much better music or any better dancing than was to be found at the large garrisons of the frontier.'[3] The melodies delighted enlisted men, officers and their families. They also brought enjoyment to the local populace who were fortunate enough to hear these artists. Army bands, as a consequence, did much to foster good relations between the troops and their civilian neighbors. Such exchanges drew the two segments of society closer together, rather than encourag-

ing isolation between them.[4] Military musicians likewise lent pomp to a number of martial ceremonies ranging from parades to guard mounts. Weddings and funerals also demanded their talents. These men helped maintain rituals important to their superiors and contributed to the morale and *esprit* of their comrades in arms.

Beyond the immediate effect of these bandsmen, one can only ponder about their influence on the development of American music. They transported a special type of culture even to remote areas, for a diverse audience who might not otherwise have come to appreciate such pursuits.[5] Despite their prominent place in the cultural history of the Trans-Mississippi West during the years between 1866 and 1902, only minor attention has been paid to the Army bands.[6]

The next few pages represent an attempt to expand the awareness about this rather neglected aspect of American military history. The activities of bands, their music, and even their instrumentation all deserve exploration. This preliminary study will hopefully satisfy the casual reader's curiosity and stimulate further research by serious scholars.

The authors' research led them to many places; for example, the state historical societies of Arizona, California, Kansas, Montana, Nebraska, New Mexico, North Dakota, South Dakota, Utah and Wyoming required visits or correspondence. Furthermore, the Presidio Army Museum in San Francisco and the nearby Society of California Pioneers proved helpful, as did the US Cavalry Museum at Fort Riley, Fort Leavenworth's historical museum, the University of Kansas

Library's Special Collections and, of course, the National Archives. Secondary sources were made possible through the interlibrary loan capabilities of Fort Hays State University's Forsyth Library and the Farrel Library of Kansas State University.

In addition to these institutions, a number of individuals gave assistance, including B. William Henry, of the National Park Service Jefferson National Memorial in St. Louis; Thomas Lindmier, curator of Fort Bridger State Historic Site and Museum in Wyoming; Franklin Smith, dedicated student of military music; Dr. Francis Lord, long-time researcher of the Civil War; Jacques Noel Jacobsen Jr., military antique dealer and editor; Dr. James Wengert, historian, musician and good friend; Mark Elrod, respected writer on Civil War military music; Dr. Homer Socolofsky, professor of history at Kansas State University, who introduced the authors to each other by long distance; and Dr. Don Rickey Jr., noted scholar of the frontier army. Finally, Dr. Leo Oliva and Professor Lyle Dilley deserve special credit. To these last three individuals the authors dedicate this publication.

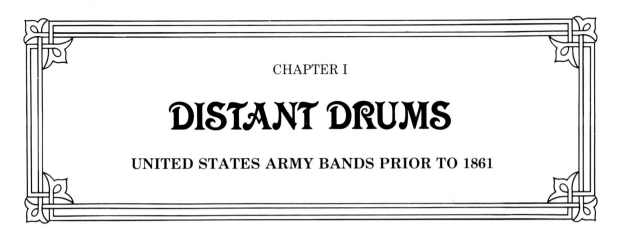

CHAPTER I

DISTANT DRUMS

UNITED STATES ARMY BANDS PRIOR TO 1861

The history of American military bands dates from the earliest days of the Revolution. There were probably a few fife and drum corps prior to the Revolution, but little information of these has been found.[1] Although it was formerly believed that the bands of that period were nothing more than the previously mentioned fife and drum corps, there is evidence to the contrary.[2] In his book on early American concert life, Oscar G. Sonneck mentioned bands 'consisting of clarinets, flutes, French horns, bassoons, etc'[3] while a Virginia regiment in the Continental Army boasted a band of '4 clarinets doubling violins, 2 bassoons doubling bass viol, and 3 horns.'[4]

These bands were entirely unofficial and were usually paid for by subscriptions from officers of the army,[5] and their primary function was to entertain the officers who had contributed to their maintenance, the task of signaling being given over to the fifes and drums.[6] Occasionally, bands gave public concerts or played for dances.[7] Other functions included music for ceremonies, parades, funerals, executions and recruiting activities, and greeting arriving detachments of troops.[8]

Because officers, rather than the public treasury, financed the bands, requests by superiors for bands' services often proved a source of discontentment. A case in point involved General George Washington's request, in February 1779, for one of his subordinates to provide a band for ceremonies celebrating the signing of the French alliance of the previous year. When Washington ordered one of the two regimental commanders who had bands to begin preparations for the event, that officer refused on the grounds that

he and his fellow officers, not Washington, had financed the creation and existence of the band. After much foot-dragging and parsimony, the band eventually began preparations for the event. The group ultimately escaped final responsibility, however, because it was short of several players and Washington was determined to have nothing but a complete band. He told the go-between to forget the whole matter and procured the services of a third band, making the man in the middle furious due to the damage to his ego.[9]

After the Revolution, bands continued to exist under a semi-official status induced by the provisions of various Army enabling acts for musicians. Although it was implied that these musicians were primarily fifers and drummers, there is little reason to believe that some could not have been performers on other instruments.[10] Upon creation of the 2nd Infantry Regiment in 1791, no band was authorized. However, a reorganization of the Army in 1796 and the death of General Anthony Wayne brought General James Wilkinson to the position of Commanding General. As one of his first official acts, he ordered the Quartermaster General to purchase instruments for the purpose of forming a band. A little over a year later, this band had been organized and was ready to assume its duties, which included performing 'on the grand parade at morning and evening roll call when the weather is fair while the parade is forming, and the guards are until further orders to be marched off to this music.' The 2nd Infantry Band remains to this day as one of the three oldest bands in the military service of the United States, the other organizations being the Corps of Artillery

Band, formed in 1795, and the United States Marine Band, formed in 1798.[11]

During the War of 1812, few changes took place in the development of music in the Army. The notable exception was a gradual shift from fifes and drums to bugles as a means of conveying signals. Little information concerning specific bands and their activities has been located. It appears, however, that most bands were attached to militia units as was the case during the Revolution.[12]

Following the War of 1812, the United States entered upon a thirty-year period of peace, broken only by occasional isolated encounters with various Indian tribes. During this interval, the growth of Army bands received several well-deserved boosts. In 1821, the protests of Secretary of War John C. Calhoun notwithstanding, Congress cut the size of the Army to 6,600 men, but this action failed to affect the quasi-official status of bands as the number and size of those in existence at the time remained unchanged. At the same time, bands received their first official recognition, and they were authorized to be formed as a separate squad in each regiment, responsible to the adjutant.[13]

In the Army Regulations of 1825, provision was made for the first time to finance bands in a manner other than out of officers' pockets: the creation of a regimental fund, derived from a 5 percent tax on sutlers' (contract storekeepers') sales, was authorized. Regulations earmarked a portion of this fund for the support of bands, but no dollar figure for the amount realized was given. In addition, the same regulations directed that bands were to be combined with the drums of the regimental field music to form a complete musical entity.[14]

What has generally been interpreted as a setback, but which may really have been a move toward permanence in the development of army bands, occurred in 1832. Army Regulations of that year specified that regimental bands were to be limited in size to ten members plus the chief musician (leader) authorized by law; in addition, the bandsmen were made liable for regular military training and service in the ranks should the need arise.[15]

During the Mexican War in 1847, however, the size of bands was increased to sixteen players, who were again to be mustered in a separate squad but were also liable to be called upon for service in the ranks.[16] To date, however, research has uncovered nothing concerning the role of bands during the war. William Carter White, in his work on the history of American military music, says that bands were evidently scattered about the Army with bandsmen performing as stretcher bearers, field messengers, and water carriers. He cited a letter of one army bandmaster which said that his band did not play a note during the entire war.[17]

During peacetime, however, bands probably performed similar functions in the 1848–61 period to those during the last four decades of the nineteenth century, which means that they provided music for military ceremonies.[18] They also entertained the troops and local population, as evidenced by the statement that the 6th Infantry Band delighted the people of Minnesota with its concerts consisting of 'selections from the standard operas and the "highly artificial" compositions of Bellini, Rossini, and others.'[19] During times of boredom or hardship the bandsmen also attempted to cheer up their comrades. When the 2nd US Cavalry moved west, in 1855, they traveled in bitter weather. On Christmas Eve the Regimental Band hoped to boost spirits by serenading the regimental commander and his wife with instrumentals and Swiss yodeling.[20]

CHAPTER II

KEEP STEP WITH THE UNION

CIVIL WAR BANDS

At the beginning of the Civil War there were few military bands. Among those in existence, however, were the United States Marine Band, several Regular Army regimental bands, the United States Military Academy Band, and bands associated with various state and local militia units. Some of these militia bands were of high quality because adequate funds to hire trained musicians, both as players and as leaders, were available.[1] Among the bands of outstanding abilities were that of the 7th New York Infantry, led by Claudio S. Grafulla; the 24th Massachusetts Infantry, led by Patrick S. Gilmore; and the American Brass Band of Providence, Rhode Island, attached to the 1st Rhode Island Infantry and led by Joseph Green.[2] Within a few months, however, additional bands were organized after Congress authorized the creation of regimental bands for the Regular Army.[3]

The purpose of the law was carried out on 31 July 1861, when War Department General Order No. 48 was published. This order specified that each infantry regiment (sixteen or twenty-four companies) was entitled to two musicians per company; cavalry and artillery regiments (twelve companies or batteries respectively) were also permitted to have two musicians per company or battery.[4] Orders further specified that each infantry regiment was entitled to have among its ranks one drum major or leader for the band and two principal musicians, each cavalry regiment two chief buglers, and each artillery regiment two principal musicians. Bands were limited in size, with those of infantry and artillery regiments restricted to twenty-four members and those of

cavalry regiments to sixteen members.[5] Although there appeared to be a conflict between the number of musicians authorized per company and the size set for the band, such was not the case because some of the authorized musicians were assigned to the field music. This situation came about since the term 'musician' as used in 1861 referred not to bandsmen, but rather to the field music, *i.e.* fifes (or bugles) and drums. The two groups constituted entirely separate entities and performed different functions. The bands primarily provided entertainment; the field music offered signals and ceremonial music.

The manner in which the bandsmen were to be paid was also specified in this order:

> One-fourth of each the pay and allowances of sergeants of engineer soldiers; one-fourth, those of corporals of engineer soldiers; and one-half, those of engineer soldiers of the first class. The drum major or leader of the band, the pay and emoluments of a second lieutenant of infantry.[6]

According to a report compiled by the Paymaster General of the Army in response to an 1862 congressional inquiry, first-class musicians were paid $34.00 per month, second-class musicians earned $20.00 per month, and third-class musicians obtained $17.00 per month; moreover, drum majors received $105.50 per month.[7] In addition to basic salaries, costs of clothing, equipment, transportation, and subsistence were also provided, but the rates of allowance for these items were not given.

With the rapid increase in size of the Army, especially with the proliferation of volunteer regiments provided by the States and whose expenses after mustering in were assumed by the Federal Government, some members of Congress became increasingly cost-conscious. They evidently felt that the cost of maintaining bands for all regiments was becoming excessive, since on 31 January 1862 the House of Representatives adopted the following resolution:

> *Resolved*, that the Secretary of War be requested to inform the House how many regimental bands are now in the service of the United States, what the cost is to the Government of each band, and whether the services of such bands cannot be dispensed without injury to the public service.[8]

In response to inquiries by Secretary of War Simon Cameron, the Adjutant, Paymaster, Quartermaster, and Commissary generals prepared a joint report. It showed that the average cost of maintaining an artillery or cavalry band for one year was $9,161.30, and that the cost of maintaining the larger infantry band for one year was $13,139.40. Included in these totals were salaries of members, clothing, equipment, transportation, and subsistence.[9]

Another portion of the same report gave, insofar as possible, the number of regiments in the service of the United States and whether or not each had a band. In the Regular Army twenty-six of the thirty regiments had bands, and incomplete data concerning the volunteer regiments supplied by the various States showed 465 regiments and 213 bands.[10] From this data, the Secretary of War concluded that the bands were overly expensive and could be disposed of without injury to the service. He transmitted this information to Galusha Grow, the Speaker of the House of Representatives.[11] It undoubtedly became the basis for Public Law 165, passed on 17 July 1862, which abolished regimental bands in the volunteer service and provided for the mustering out of all musicians therein within thirty days.[12] It must be noted that this act applied only to bands in the volunteer service and not to bands of the Regular Army.

The abolition of regimental bands in the volunteer service did not, however, mean that the Army was to be entirely deprived of bands' services and benefits. On the contrary, bands remained an integral part of the service, and the act also provided that musicians in regimental bands might be transferred to newly authorized brigade bands, provided that a bandsman's original enlistment had been as a musician. Otherwise the bandsmen were either to be mustered out or transferred to combat duty.[13]

Since four or more regiments made up a brigade, this practice probably cut the number of bands from 239 to approximately 60.[14] Unfortunately, no exact data are available because brigades were often transferred from one division to another throughout their period of service. One historian, Francis A. Lord, stated that in the records at the National Archives, sixty brigade bands have been positively identified and that the list which he compiled was by no means complete.[15]

Public Law 165 also set the number of players in all bands at sixteen. Players' pay remained unchanged, with the exception of that of leaders. Leaders' pay was cut from $105.50 per month to $45.00 plus allowances equal to those of quartermaster sergeants.[16]

Prior to the action of Congress, Adjutant General Lorenzo Thomas had already acted to halt the proliferation of bands. In General Order No. 91, dated 26 October 1861, he prohibited the mustering in of any more bands for volunteer regiments. In addition, he also ordered that any vacancies which might occur in these bands were not to be filled and that all nonmusicians who might belong to them were to be discharged immediately upon receipt of the order.[17]

The effect of these policy changes on the quality of bands and band music during the war cannot be ascertained from the sources now available. However, if the attitude which Congress showed toward the Army in times of peace throughout the nineteenth century was any indication, the bands probably suffered. On the other hand, the elimination of poor musicians from musical organizations almost always brings a corresponding increase in quality. Bell Wiley, a noted Civil War scholar, in his book *The Life of Billy Yank*, gave that impression and also noted that the men generally appreciated good music.[18]

That appreciation for the benefits of good music was best expressed by a soldier of the 24th Massachusetts Infantry in April 1862. He wrote a letter home complimenting the regimental band and its leader Patrick S. Gilmore for their 'splendid concerts, playing selections from the opera and some very pretty marches, quicksteps, waltzes and the like, most of which are composed by himself or by Ferdinand Zohler, a member of the band.'[19]

Good bands often found that their services

were much in demand. Among their duties was that of serenading officers. Although these serenades (concerts in modern terminology) were for the benefit of the officers, there was no way to prevent the rank-and-file soldiers from listening and enjoying the music.[20] Sometimes these serenades became regular musical marathons, taxing the players' endurance. In the last month of the war, General Samuel D. Sturgis, who in the postwar period became Colonel of the 7th Cavalry, had his brigade band play for six hours without a break, from 8.00 p.m. one night until 2.00 a.m. the next morning.[21] Another example of overdone serenading took place in June 1863, during the Gettysburg campaign. On that occasion one band serenaded a general in the morning, a second general in the afternoon, and a third general in the evening.[22] Probably the most humorous example of an ill-considered serenade took place late in the war when an Illinois band was requested by a staff officer to serenade what was believed to be a 'Female Seminary.' Permission was granted and the serenade began, to be terminated when staff members of the 'Seminary' politely informed the officer that the music was unheard and therefore unappreciated by the deaf-mute residents of the institution.[23]

Strange though it may seem, in many instances bands accompanied troops into battle, playing all the while. During General George B. McClellan's Peninsular Campaign of 1862, the band of the 10th Massachusetts Infantry came under heavy fire at Fair Oaks and at least one musician was wounded.[24] At Williamsburg (5 May 1862) an unidentified band received credit for stemming an ill-timed retreat. As the soldiers began to run toward the rear, their commander, seeing that his orders for them to halt were in vain, and noticing some bandsmen nearby, ordered 'Halt there! Halt! Give us Yankee Doodle or some other doodle!' Although the tune which the band struck up was not 'Yankee Doodle,' it did have the desired effect.[25]

At Antietam (16–17 September 1862) another unidentified band actually accompanied troops into action. According to Confederate General John B. Gordon, the attack consisted of four lines of battle and the 'magnificent array moved to the charge, every step keeping time to the tap of the deep-sounding drum.'[26] At Chancellorsville (1–4 May 1863) several Union bands performed heroically in an attempt to prevent the disaster threatened

by Confederate General Stonewall Jackson's surprise attack. Union General Winfield Scott Hancock ordered every band present to play 'Rally Round the Flag,' and they did so despite the fact that shells were falling all around them. The band of the 14th Connecticut Infantry even went into the space between the opposing forces and played patriotic tunes such as 'The Star Spangled Banner' and 'Yankee Doodle,' a task which undoubtedly required nerves of steel, and emerged without any major casualties. This performance had the desired effect of calming the pandemonium caused by the flight of the 11th Corps, demoralized as it was by Jackson's attack.[27]

Probably the most important of the official duties of bands was that of providing music for dress parades. Parades formed an important facet of military life: as a test of efficiency of training and organization, they ranked second only to combat experience because they let commanders observe the actions of their troops while under pressure. The parade served both as a means of inspection of the soldier and his reaction to his training, and as a means of bringing daily activities to a close. After initial preparations, the troops would form, and then the band would strike up some spirited tune to whose accompaniment the companies and regiments filed past the reviewing officers in perfect order.[28] The charm and spirit of such a parade often depended upon the caliber of the bands of the participating organizations. If the bandsmen were good, the parade usually went off without any problems, but if the musicians were poor (and many were), things often went to pieces. Even though musical quality was sometimes lacking, the spirit with which the bandsmen applied themselves to the music probably made up for a few wrong notes and missed beats.[29]

Other circumstances in which bands played an important part arose when a camp moved. As soon as preparations for the shift had been completed, the various bands were ordered into position to lead the units out of the bivouac area.[30] The music could also be a great reviver. A catchy tune or a stirring march generally caused even the weariest soldier to lift his head and stride along as though he had just begun a day's march instead of having been on the road all day.

Morale always presented a problem in any military force and nowhere was this truer than in hospitals. In an effort to bolster spirits during the Civil War, Union officials decided to station bands in some of the larger hospitals. Mower General Hospital in Philadelphia, for example, had its own parade ground and bandstand where bands and drum corps played daily. Officialdom apparently felt that patients would hear the music of the bands and forget their suffering.[31] In addition to their musical duties, musicians stationed in or near hospitals usually took on additional detail to assist in medical work, serving as orderlies, as stretcher-bearers on battlefields, and as kitchen police. The same function often applied to bands associated with combat troops.[32]

It would appear, therefore, that bands did perform valuable services in the promulgation of the war effort, notwithstanding the protests of certain officials about the high cost of maintaining them. It would be impossible to calculate their exact impact, but if they only served to cheer up one demoralized soldier, the cost which the government incurred was undoubtedly worthwhile.[33]

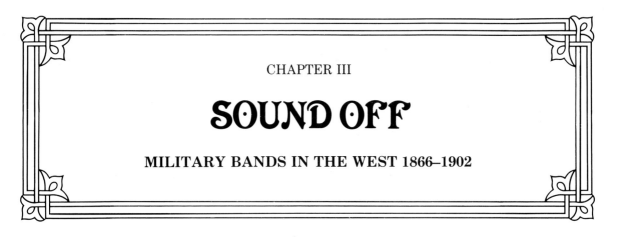

CHAPTER III

SOUND OFF

MILITARY BANDS IN THE WEST 1866–1902

In her preface to *Following the Guidon*, Elizabeth B. Custer noted that the bugle 'was the hourly monitor of the cavalry corps. It told us when to eat, to sleep, to march, and to go to church.' In fact, nearly every aspect of daily life was governed 'by its clarion notes,' so that the frontier soldier 'needed timepieces only when absent from garrison or camp.'[1] Mrs. Custer could well have stated that even in the field the bugles went along with the men – both horse soldiers and foot troops alike. Not only did the bugler accompany his comrades everywhere, but the regimental band sometimes left the post on campaign as well.

Whether at the fort or on the march the United States Army carried music with it to the Trans-Mississippi West. At Washita Custer's 7th Cavalry band played in the freezing cold. In 1869, when the golden spike tied the nation together at Promontory Point, Utah, the 21st Infantry Band helped to celebrate the historic event. Leading dress parades, enlivening patriotic festivities, performing for dances, providing concerts, and escorting funerals kept martial musicians busy and brought a certain amount of pomp, entertainment, and culture to remote areas of the frontier.

Bands became extremely popular then, for the Army and for local civilians as well. One nineteenth century observer went so far as to say that 'there can be no comparison between the really inspiring qualities of a band of music,' and 'the dubious benefit' of fancy uniforms to impress the public. The writer, Lieutenant Charles DeLano Hine, continued that a band was 'attractive to the community at large, and in various ways helps to bring the

Army in touch with the people.'[2] Others agreed with Hine's pronouncement. Some commanders thought so highly of a band's potential to promote *esprit* and public relations that they went to great lengths to ensure success. Colonel Benjamin Grierson, the commander of the 10th US Cavalry and an accomplished musician himself, restricted band membership to men who could read, write and seemed capable of learning music. Since literate individuals were in short supply, Grierson's standards for regimental bandsmen were high. The Colonel also established a band fund to support the purchase of instruments, sheet music and related items. Each soldier was asked to contribute fifty cents, while each group of company officers was requested to donate fifty dollars.[3] Since a private made only $13 per month and a young lieutenant lived on a base pay of $125 per month, the sum was affordable, yet substantial.

The 7th Cavalry likewise used a similar method to raise funds, and soon collected $959.[4] The requirement to solicit money from the rank and file indicated the need for a better means of financing bands. Regimental funds were established to this end. According to the 1873 Revised Army Regulations these were to be used exclusively for the maintenance of the band and the establishment of post libraries.[5] Supposedly the revenue came through the sale of surplus foodstuffs and rations. Since the military fare proved meager in the decades following the Civil War, critics questioned why music and books took precedence over the enlisted men's stomachs.

In an effort to overcome such criticism regimental commanders wrestled with other means to obtain revenue. Some offered new ideas to resolve the long-standing problem of finance. One of the most novel solutions came from Colonel Delancy Floyd-Jones of the 3rd Infantry. The Colonel suggested that a percentage of the fines imposed by regimental courts-martial be paid to the regimental funds for the support of bands. He stated that many officers not stationed at regimental headquarters, where the bands were located, did not benefit from contributing to the upkeep of the musical program. Since the fines imposed were supposedly being donated to charity, the Colonel reasoned that regimental funds should absorb the cash, and the Army would thereby reap the benefits.[6] Despite its merits the idea failed to gain approval.

If legislation to finance musical efforts caused distress, sanction for the existence of the bands themselves proved equally as frustrating. Despite a longstanding tradition for the existence of Army bands, and especially because of noteworthy service between 1861 and 1865, the retention of these organizations would seem inevitable after Appomatox. This supposition did not prove the case. Bands fell victim to the drastic cutbacks which appeared under the Army Reorganization Act of 1866. Infantry regiments could field only 20 musicians and two principal musicians, while artillery units boasted 24 musicians and the same number of principal musicians as authorized for the infantry. The same legislation did away with bands for cavalry regiments, and replaced them with 24 trumpeters and one chief.[7]

Official elimination of the cavalry's musical element did not mean that bands actually disappeared from that branch. While in some cases the organization was abolished and the members discharged (as occurred in the 2nd Cavalry), most regiments found a way to keep their bandsmen together.[8]

Eventually, the authorities in Washington relented. Cavalry bands, along with the other combat arms, ultimately stood on a more solid foundation via the timeless practice of detailing soldiers for extra duty. The Secretary of War attempted to establish martial music on an even firmer footing when he proposed that the Army be allowed to enlist bands with twenty-five members. He reasoned that, after making allowances for illness and injury, an effective strength of twenty members would be realized.[9] Unfortunately, the plan seems to have gone unheeded. In fact, the strength of

bands fell short of even the actual meager allowances of Army Regulations. In some instances the total number of musicians dropped to as low as nine men – excluding the three non-commissioned members of the band provided for by the Army Appropriation Act of 1869.[10]

Over the decades many of the bandsmen no doubt came to resent the lack of stability within their ranks. The 21st Infantry Band even went so far as to submit a petition requesting official recognition of the regimental bands. They stated that the government permitted each regiment to have a band but actually recognized only the band at the United States Military Academy. The petition admitted that provision was made for chief musicians and for detailing men for special duty in bands. It pointed out, however, that although some men did become proficient musicians, the fact that civilian employment was generally more lucrative caused most not to reenlist upon expiration of their five years of service – a problem still faced by the military in many specialties today. This rapid turnover of personnel made the work of the band leader difficult and was the chief reason that some bandsmen felt they belonged to one of 'the tabooed institutions of the civilized world.' The petition enclosed with the letter requested that the bill before Congress to reorganize the band of the Military Academy be amended so that it would apply to all bands;[11] as a result, the House Committee on Military Affairs prepared a substitute bill to include all bands.[12] Evidently, the matter never left the confines of the Committee. No legislation appeared relative to the matter save a minor Congressional concession in 1891 allowing appropriated funds to be used in the purchase of instruments.

If legal and fiscal considerations posed problems to the existence of musical organizations, the recruitment of members offered an equally knotty challenge. Men who could perform on the various types of instruments needed to create effective musical entities were scarce. Often regimental commanders faced immense difficulties in securing qualified musicians, and some went to great lengths to do so. This problem seems to have been best attacked by Colonel Grierson. As his early life had included both training in and the teaching of music, he found a few qualified musicians and personally taught others he thought possessed musical aptitude.[13]

Other officers demonstrated similar initiative. For example, the band of the 7th Cavalry was largely the creation of Major Alfred Gibbs. In a letter dated 28 April 1867 to Captain Myles Keogh, commander of Fort Wallace, Gibbs directed that any men in Keogh's company who had ever played in a brass band be sent to Fort Riley for duty in the regimental band.[14] This letter probably came about as the result of an order issued on 12 April 1867. The missive from Colonel A. J. Smith, commander of the regiment, directed Lieutenant Colonel George A. Custer to designate fifteen enlisted men as members of the band and instructed these men to proceed to Fort Riley with Major Gibbs.[15] Smith specified that in order that the band might be 'organized and made efficient as rapidly as possible, the members of the same, on their arrival at Fort Riley, Ks., will not be subject to the ordinary details for garrison duty.'[16] Such solicitude on the part of the regimental commander undoubtedly contributed to the rapid rise of the 7th Cavalry Band to prominence as a musical organization.

Lieutenant Colonel George Crook of the 23rd Infantry attacked the problem of recruits for the band from still another angle. He felt that the best musicians were generally European immigrants. Accordingly, in a letter dated 3 May 1872 to Colonel Jefferson C. Davis, the regiment's commanding officer, he suggested that someone be sent to Castle Garden, the point of arrival for German immigrants, to recruit musicians there.[17]

Whether or not Davis followed up on Crook's suggestion cannot be ascertained. The idea, however, was not far-fetched since one descendant of a Victorian-era US Army officer contended that 'Army bands were composed almost entirely of Germans and Italians;'[18] indeed, the splendid band of the 8th Infantry was supposedly imported 'direct from Italy.'[19] While such a practice was probably not all that widespread, a few Italian names found their way into print. For example, George A. Custer's last message to his subordinates was carried by trumpeter Giovanni Martini, who at the age of fourteen served with Garibaldi as a drummer boy.[20] Another emigrant from Italy, Achilles LaGuardia (whose son Fiorello became New York City's colorful mayor), arrived in the United States to accompany an opera singer. He remained after the tour, and entered the US Army as a bandmaster with the 11th Infantry, a position he held until his death in 1898.[21]

Recruiting men from specific ethnic back-grounds seemed to indicate adherence to stereotypical views regarding musical ability. This factor also manifested itself to a certain degree within the four Black regiments. The bands of the 9th and 10th Cavalry, as well as those of the 24th and 25th Infantry, allegedly 'prided themselves in their proficiency in military exercises' and the quality of their music.[22] The fact that the 24th Infantry boasted a repertoire of about 1,000 numbers, and a music library valued at over $6,000, in the late 1890s provides some indication of how serious these black bandsmen viewed their craft.[23] Their counterparts in the 25th Infantry also performed with professional pride, and displayed no lack of showmanship; in fact, the drum major of this outfit probably initiated the use of baton twirling and gymnastics in the 1880s.[24] While such practices now seem commonplace, in the late nineteenth century these gyrations represented novelties. Even in the early twentieth century this type of performance drew attention. One observer recorded: 'At formal reviews the Drum Major of the band is an object not to be looked upon without awe.' Continuing, the writer noted that 'He wore a huge, white bearskin hat that towers above his tall head. The messenger who announced the fall of Jericho wouldn't have been half so impressive as the august, black potentate, when he turns his baton as the signal for the band to wheel past the commanding officer . . .'[25]

While the movements of the band's leader may have represented an innovation, the tall bearskin mentioned in this description had a long tradition in Army bands. Actually, non-regulation headgear abounded in these musical organizations since regulations had long authorized the commanding officer to 'make such additions in ornaments as he may judge proper' providing the council of administration sanctioned the changes and supplied the funds to procure extra uniform components.[26] This provision allowed wide latitude in the outfits worn by bands. Special headgear, additional cords and braid, custom accoutrements, extra buttons, and even made-to-order coats became the rule rather than the exception.[27] In due course each band took on a distinctive appearance: no two organizations looked exactly alike. This diversity probably went against the grain of those Army officers who opted for strict uniformity in military dress.

While Army rules governing what the bands

should wear caused some confusion, a more serious quirk existed in regulations. According to 'The Book' bandsmen were to be dropped from company rolls and mustered in a separate squad under the chief musician who reported directly to the regimental adjutant, but what about quarters? Although some posts offered adequate quarters, in many cases billets for bands were substandard or nonexistent. In 1875, Colonel George L. Andrews, the commander of the 25th Infantry, complained to the Commander of the Department of Texas that his band never had decent accommodations: during the six years they served in Texas the men lacked proper quarters, and for two years of that time, at Fort Clark, they even lived in tents.[28]

Sometimes even these makeshift facilities were absent, especially if a musician decided to become a family man. In one instance a trombone player with the 10th Infantry found himself in dire straits. His wife was due to have a baby and he 'could get no quarters.' Out of sympathy, an officer's family took the couple into their home. The wife in turn helped with household chores, particularly cooking. Because the house's walls measured three feet in thickness the young trombonist could even continue to practice and not disturb the rest of the residents.[29] This arrangement worked well for all parties involved. The young musician, because of the kindness extended by one of the regiment's officers, probably lived better than his comrades who remained in the barracks. He enjoyed a certain degree of privacy over the open bay arrangement that the other musicians found as their lot. He partook of homecooked meals which represented an improvement over the monotonous fare provided in the mess halls of the era.[30] The fortunate trombonist may also have obtained a little extra money from his wife's service to the officer's household, a welcome addition to the $13 per month pay, and if he somehow managed to attain the position of Chief Musician for the regiment he received the princely sum of $60 per month (see Table 1). In its time this salary provided considerable buying power and totaled more than double the pay of the regiment's top noncommissioned officer, the sergeant major. Unfortunately, only a select few ever achieved the coveted position. Once they earned this niche, the chief musicians understandably often remained in their jobs until retirement.

No matter who assumed leadership for the regimental band, the duties and functions kept him and his subordinates busy. Even at installations where no regimental organizations existed, extra-duty post bands sometimes formed to provide music.[31] This phenomenon most frequently arose when a fort decided to put on a dance known as a 'hop.' Some of these affairs assumed rather elaborate proportions, and made an impression on the local community as well. One example of this type of performance took place at Fort Hays, Kansas, in 1874. A newspaper captured the scene in some detail, reporting:

> An event that has long been premeditated . . . came to a successful issue last Wednesday evening: simply the grand ball given by 'C' company, Sixth cavalry. The intent was to make it stupendous and so it was. Probably no similar event has ever transpired in Western Kansas that can equal it . . . The music stand, an elaborate platform, was tastefully decorated with flags and evergreens, from which the Sixth band discoursed elaborate strains of music. There was an aggregate of two hundred couples – parties from Wallace, Ellis, Dodge, Victoria, Russell, and Ellsworth graced the fete with their presence. Hays City turned out en masse, and, in fact, the crowd was immense, and good will pervaded the entire affair.[32]

Certain daily activities such as guard mount, retreat, dress parades, and reviews demanded the presence of bands at military posts, especially at division, departmental, or regimental headquarters' posts. Each of these ceremonies had a specific function and purpose. All were similar in that each involved a formation of troops upon the parade ground of a military post. All except a review were formal processions of a body of troops before some officer in either his or the troops' honor. In each the band played a prominent role when available; if no band were available, music was then furnished by trumpets and drums.

For example, on 8 June 1869 Major Eugene Asa Carr led the 5th Cavalry out of Fort McPherson, Nebraska, to begin a campaign against the Sioux and Cheyenne. The command passed in review before General C. C. Augur, commander of the Department of the Platte, and Brevet Brigadier General Thomas Duncan, commander of the post. On that occasion 'drums rolled', and the band provided martial music.[33]

The 7th Cavalry also participated in its share of reviews. Twice after the Washita

TABLE 1
PAY OF BANDSMEN UNDER THE PAY ACT OF 1872 ($)

		Year 1	Year 2	Year 3	Year 4	Year 5
First Enlistment	Enlisted Musician	13	13	14	15	16
	Principal Musician	22	22	23	24	25
Second Enlistment	Enlisted Musician	18	18	18	18	18
	Principal Musician	27	27	27	27	27
Third Enlistment	Enlisted Musician	19	19	19	19	19
	Principal Musician	28	28	28	28	28
Fourth Enlistment	Enlisted Musician	20	20	20	20	20
	Principal Musician	29	29	29	29	29
Fifth Enlistment	Enlisted Musician	21	21	21	21	21
	Principal Musician	30	30	30	30	30

Chief Musicians were paid a flat rate of $60 per month; other amounts are monthly rates. Sources: US Congress, House, House Executive Document No. 1, Pt. II; Secretary of War, *Annual Report, 1875*, 44th Cong., 1st sess., I, p. 359.

campaign the unit rode to the strains of 'Garry Owen.' In 1868 their own band did the honors, and in the next year Colonel Nelson A. Miles' 5th Infantry Band supplied the music.[34] Some twenty-two years later the 7th again took part in a victory review for Miles at Pine Ridge Agency. By now the officer was a general. Again, the program included 'Garry Owen.'[35]

Akin to the review, but of greater importance, was the dress parade. This generally took place each afternoon and served as a means for commanders to inspect their commands and to disseminate necessary orders and information. These had a certain ritual which was observed scrupulously because a poor parade reflected negatively upon the participants. In these parades the band, or the field music if no band were available or if the weather were bad, played an important role.

When the call 'Assembly' was sounded by the buglers or trumpeters of the command, the command formed on the parade ground according to a specified formula with all participants located at specified intervals. The band was stationed to the right of the line of troops. As soon as the parade was formed, the band played and marched in front of the company commanders from right to left and back to its post. After reports were given by noncommissioned officers to their commanders and by the commanders to the adjutant, orders were issued and the command was inspected. Then the parade was dismissed. As the companies left the parade ground, the band played until all were off the field, when it too returned to its quarters. This ritual, although formal and set by prescribed rules, was subject to occasional variance. The most notable deviation was that,

when the parade was small, the band might play to the left in common or quick time.[36]

A function of bands not recognized by many was that of providing a means of passing some of the off-duty hours the soldiers possessed. A report in a military periodical in 1886 paid tribute to Lieutenant M. O. Parker of the 10th Cavalry for organizing a band at Fort Washakie, Wyoming Territory, to help the men 'to while away the long winter evenings and break the monotony of garrison routine.'[37] It appears from the meager evidence available that this band was primarily an extra-duty organization, but it may also have performed some of the duties required by army regulations and routine.

Army regulations specified that when one or more companies of a regiment were stationed at headquarters, the band was also to be located there. Those same regulations also stated that 'When practicable, regimental bands will be sent, for short periods of time, to different posts occupied by companies of the regiment.'[38] The arrival of regimental bands on these tours offered excellent entertainment for troops stationed at outlying posts. The bands usually spent two or three weeks there playing for dances and concerts. In 1878, the band of the 19th Infantry visited Fort Supply, Indian Territory, and in 1879 and 1880 the bands of the 23rd and the 24th Infantry Regiments were stationed there.[39]

Band concerts took place frequently. Both the troops and the civilians associated with the posts where bands were stationed enjoyed these performances. Many references to band concerts appear in newspapers published in towns adjacent to military posts. For example, the Hays City *Sentinel* of 22 March 1876 carried a notice asking why the band at the post could not give a concert. The editor felt certain that the citizens would appreciate such a musical treat as the 5th Cavalry Orchestra would give.

From October 1879 to November 1880, when the 4th Cavalry band served at Fort Hays, it gave weekly concerts. On 17 November 1879 the Ellis County *Star* carried an article about a concert given the previous Sunday evening. The reporter found the music delightful. On 4 December the editor of the *Star* wrote that 'delicious strains of music come wafted [sic] to our ear from the direction of the post.' On 9 January 1880 the editor of the *Sentinel* commented:

> The rendition of airs from the opera of Martha [sic] by the Fourth Cavalry band last Monday was remarkably fine. At the Sunday concert some rare melodies from 'Tannhauser' [sic] called forth unbounded praise from judges of good music.

Concerts offered more than entertainment since in some instances they honored various visiting dignitaries and officers from other posts. In 1875 a party of several officers and Secretary of War William W. Belknap, who were on a tour to Yellowstone National Park, received recognition at Fort Sanders, Wyoming Territory. The 2nd Cavalry Band gave a concert in Secretary Belknap's honor.[40]

The party heard other bands at several posts which they visited in the course of their journey. On 20 July musicians of the 14th Infantry serenaded the Secretary at Fort Douglas, Utah Territory. The band played for over two hours. On 31 August, on the return trip to Chicago, Colonel William B. Hazen of the 6th Infantry and the regimental band greeted the group upon their arrival at Fort Buford, Dakota Territory. General William E. Strong, retired Inspector General of the Freedman's Bureau, who penned an account of the journey, thought that this was 'the best band we have heard on the trip.'[41]

Army Regulations of the late nineteenth century were less restrictive than those of the present time concerning nonmilitary duties of the various components of the service. Thus, one finds bands taking part in nonmilitary public and private functions on a regular basis. Indeed, in September 1883, bands were very much in evidence during Henry Villard's excursion to celebrate the completion of the Northern Pacific Railroad. The entourage passed through Billings on 7 September, pausing long enough for several railway and political dignitaries to tour the city, give short speeches, and be entertained by the 2nd Cavalry Band, then stationed at nearby Fort Custer. 'The music furnished by the . . . band . . . was appreciated not only by the citizens of the town, but by the excursionists.' Those responsible for the performance 'won golden opinions not only for the music . . . but also for the spirit with which they entered into the celebration.'[42]

From Billings the excursion continued west toward Gold Creek, the site of the junction of the rails. Among the entourage was the 5th US Infantry Band from Fort Keogh, Montana. The ceremony celebrating the junction took place on 8 September. To open the program, the 5th Infantry Band played a selection composed specially for the occasion by Chief Musician Kenneth Price. Entitled 'Grand Triumphal March "Iron Horse",' the number was designed to feature the whistle of one of the locomotives, 'but the scream of the locomotive,' in the words of a correspondent for the Helena *Daily Herald*, 'like that of the eagle's, was not attuned to the melody of the *Star Spangled Banner* or the symphonies of Mozart, so the harsh sound of the whistle . . . was silenced and the band completed their beautiful opening piece.'[43] Among other numbers on the program were compositions by Sir Arthur Sullivan, Waldteufel, and Suppé. The Suppé overture 'Morn, Noon and Night' is a staple feature of park band concerts even today.[44]

These were neither the first nor the last times that Army bands had been associated with transcontinental railroads. As noted previously, the 21st Infantry Band had been present at the junction of the Union Pacific and Central Pacific Railroads on 10 May 1869. This had happened purely by chance as the 21st Infantry was in the midst of a cross-country transfer and had just happened to hit Promontory Point on the day before the rails joined.

Nor were bands limited to participation in ceremonies marking the completion of these rail lines. Bands even accompanied troops detailed to guard railway construction crews. In the archives of the Burlington Northern Railroad is a photograph of what may be either the 6th or the 15th Infantry Band on a construction train flatcar. Among the instruments clearly visible are a cornet, a tuba, and a bass drum.

Examples of other nonmilitary functions included performances at University commencement exercises, openings of new businesses, and political and livestock growers' conventions. The 5th Infantry Band was stationed at Fort Leavenworth in 1876. In June the band journeyed 30 miles to Lawrence to participate in commencement activities at the University of Kansas. The band provided music for the processional in addition to selections between the graduation orations. In the evening a concert consisting of twelve selections was performed in the university chapel:

CONCERT PROGRAMME

PART I

March 'Jubiluani'	Faust
Selection 'Puritan's Daughter'	Balfe
Waltz 'Anna Bertha'	Marshall
Overture 'Poet and Peasant'	Suppé
Potpourri of Irish Airs:	
'Patrick's Day'	Marshall
Overture 'Norma'	Bellini

PART II

March Minnehaha	Bach
Waltz 'Binetten'	Faust
Selection 'I Puritani'	Bellini
Fantasia Mexicaine 'D'Jenika'	Bouilloun
Polonaise 'Scandinavian'	Wolfert
Galop 'Always Jolly'	Zickoff

H. A. Marshall, Leader[45]

Perhaps the most unusual performance by a regimental band took place in Miles City on 14 May 1890. The occasion was the annual convention of the Eastern Montana Woolgrowers Association and the band was that of the 22nd Infantry stationed at Fort Keogh. The program was notable because every number was somehow related to sheep and/or the sheep and wool industry. Selections played were:

'Frisky Lambs'	Neill
'Mutton March'	Daley
'The Mumming Spindles'	Gruwell
'Shearing Waltz'	Parkhurst
'Drowsy Tinkling Lulls the	
Distant Fold'	J. S. Day

Perhaps none of those in the audience realized how hard the band leader must have searched to locate selections whose titles related to the topic at hand.[46]

Sometimes the bands played at other 'road' engagements of a more exotic nature. For example, hunting parties for visiting dignitaries on occasion called upon the talents of bands for entertainment. In 1872, General Sheridan entertained a rather noteworthy guest, the Grand Duke Alexis, son of the Russian Czar. From Fort McPherson, Nebraska, the party traveled southward toward the Republican River. On 14 January 1872 it arrived at a location known as Camp Alexis on Red Willow Creek, a tributary of the Republican. William W. Tucker, a member of the party, described the arrival:

> Just before the sun had sunk below the distant hills, and as we ascended some rising ground, we were in full sight of a splendid military camp. The Stars and Stripes were seen flying from a towering flagstaff on the bank of Red Willow Creek. A cheer rose from every member of our party as this scene burst upon our sight. A few minutes more and the band of the Second Cavalry was playing the Russian Hymn, while Sheridan assisted to alight the honored guest of this magnificent camp, which bears his imperial name.[47]

A few weeks later the entourage arrived at Fort Wallace, Kansas, on its return trip East. There two companies of the 3rd Infantry and the regimental band met them. This group 'tendered a serenade during the few minutes the train remained.'[48]

Other occasions for the music of bands included funerals. In 1889 the band of the 25th Infantry (a black regiment) preceded even the Masons in the funeral cortege of Captain C. P. Higgins, a prominent citizen of Missoula, Montana.[49] Not only notable civilians went to their graves with an Army band accompaniment. Many a soldier of low rank was laid to rest in the same way described by an officer's wife: 'The adjutant of the battalion read the burial service, and the trumpeters stepped to the edge of the graves and sounded taps, which echoed sad and melancholy over those parched and arid lands.' After the conclusion of the service the music turned to 'the gay strains of "The Girl I Left Behind Me," which the trumpeters were playing with all their might.' Shocked at this outburst, the officer's lady turned to her husband for an explanation. He replied: 'You see . . . it would not do for the soldiers to be sad when one dies. Why, it would demoralize the whole command. So they play these gay things to cheer them up.'[50]

Next to funerals probably one of the most touching situations involving bands took place as a unit departed for campaign. In 1876, when the 7th Cavalry rode out of Fort Abraham Lincoln, the band did its duty. As the outfit left, a familiar tune brought tears to many eyes:

> It was a relief to escape from them and enter the garrison, and yet, when our band struck up 'The Girl I Left Behind Me,' the most despairing hour seemed to have come. All the sadfaced wives of the officers who had forced themselves to their doors to try to wave a courageous farewell and smile bravely to keep the ones they loved from knowing the anguish of their breaking hearts gave up the struggle at the sound of the music.[51]

Melancholy also accompanied many transfers. Often the people of the region where a regiment was stationed grew attached to the units in their midst and parted with them sadly. Such was the case in 1884 when the 21st Infantry left Fort Vancouver, Washington. As a local newspaper reported, 'The band played once more one of its finest pieces and then the crowd dispersed. The people having by words expressed their kindly regard for the Twenty-first from which they part with regret.'[52]

Two years later a crowd of over 1,000 gathered at Cheyenne, Wyoming Territory, to send off the 9th Infantry. After having spent seventeen years at Fort D. A. Russell, the regiment was being sent to Arizona and New Mexico. As its last act of goodwill, the 9th Infantry Band played 'Auld Lang Syne.'[53]

Fortunately, not all occasions were so solemn. Army bands enjoyed happier duties such as patriotic celebrations, social functions, fund-raising activities and even musical competitions. At least in one instance the 3rd Infantry Band went to an agricultural fair held in Denver where they competed for a $300 prize. While in Denver the musicians performed a concert in the city at Sigl's Hall. According to the *Rocky Mountain News*, the public response was favorable. Many people attended, and felt the music was performed well.[54]

Actually, the local populace displayed appreciation to these soldier-musicians in almost every instance. The only moments of discord come on those rare occasions when civilian counterparts existed. Sometimes these individuals complained that a military band took away paying customers when they provided their service free of charge. The muscian's union in San Francisco made this charge on at least one occasion.[55]

Such disgruntled comments probably were few and far between. For the most part citizens showed their approval for Army bands, as did the military community itself. Indeed, the novelist-officer Charles King captured the feelings of many Army people in this true scene from his career:

> The sun was setting in a cloudless sky as I reined in my horse in front of General Carr's quarters and dismounted to make my report of the three days hunt along the valley of the Saline for stampeded horses. The band, in neat summer dress, were grouped around the flagstaff, while the strains of 'Soldaten Lieder' thrilled through the soft evening air, and fairly carried away by the cadence of the sweet music, a party of young ladies and officers had dropped their croquet mallets and were waltzing upon the green carpet of the parade. Seated upon the verandas, other ladies and older officers were smilingly watching the pretty scene.[56]

The serene picture ably demonstrated the appreciation for music which Army bands helped to foster in the West. These bandsman, therefore, performed valuable services throughout the years after the Civil War. The poet Walt Whitman paid the finest tribute to these early musicians in the West. After hearing the 17th Infantry Band at a post in Dakota Territory, Whitman penned an important few phrases. More than anything else this poem provides insight into the feelings military bands must have stirred in many a frontier audience:

ITALIAN MUSIC IN DAKOTA
['The Seventeenth – the finest Regimental Band I ever heard']

Through the soft evening air enwinding all,
Rocks, woods, fort, cannon, pacing sentries,
  endless wilds,
In dulcet streams, in flutes' and cornets' notes,
Electric, pensive, turbulent, artificial,
(Yet strangely fitting even here, meanings
  unknown before,
Subtler than ever, more harmony, as if born
  here, related here,
Not to the city's fresco'd rooms, not to the
  audience of the opera house,
Sounds, echoes, wandering strains, as really
  here at home,
Sonnambula's innocent love, trios with
  Norma's anguish,
And thy ecstatic chorus Poliuto;)
Rayed in the limpid yellow slanting sundown,
Music, Italian music in Dakota.

While Nature, sovereign of this gnarl'd
    realm,
Lurking in hidden barbaric grim recesses,
Acknowledging rapport however, far remov'd,
(As some old root or soil of earth its last-born
    flower or fruit),
Listens well pleas'd.[57]

Even Mark Twain had a backhanded way of paying tribute to military bands. While visiting Fort Missoula, Montana, in 1895 he was asked about his quip that 'there are two things I could never understand. One is the solar eclipse and the other is the countermarching of a band.' Having just witnessed a guard mounting with muscians present, Samuel Clemens replied: 'I haven't solved the band proposition even now, and as for the other count, I was modest before I was born.'[58]

THE ILLUSTRATIONS

Previous page: Grouped in a circle, the tiny band of the 16th Infantry makes music for the garrison. Special stands hold the scores while the men play. (Kansas State Historical Society, Topeka)

Left, top: The Utah Expedition of 1858–59 witnessed the mobilization of several regiments of the Regular Army, and gave rise to numerous occasions for martial music; this is the earliest known photograph depicting US Army musicians in the West, and dates from that time. The Chief Musician of the assembled infantry buglers wears nonregulation triple rows of buttons on the chest of his frock coat to set him apart from his subordinates. Several of the men have the correct sky blue tape on the fronts of their coats as prescribed for musicians of their branch. (Utah State Historical Society)

Left, center: Fort Douglas, Utah Territory's band (no doubt the 3rd California Volunteer Infantry) gathered with their instruments, including a massive drum. These men formed part of the post garrison during the Civil War, and as such were one of the Union Army musical organizations stationed furthest west. (Utah State Historical Society)

Left, bottom: An unknown Federal Army band of the 1860s poses with its young drummer boy in the center. Youths commonly served in this capacity during the Civil War, and the custom extended to the frontier and continued in the years after the war. (Wyoming State Archives, Museums and Historical Department)

Left: General James A. Blunt commanded the District of the Frontier from 1863 to 1864. His band presented a rather rag-tag appearance in contrast to their counterparts in the East. (Kansas State Historical Society, Topeka)

Below: At the conclusion of the Civil War, the US Army looked westward once again. The 'Regulars' returned to constabulary duty on the frontier, and despite the lack of official sanction, they formed bands to accompany them across the Mississippi. Here the men at Fort Harker, Kansas, turn out in 1867 with the bandsmen – probably the 7th Cavalry's musicians – mounted atop matched white horses. (Kansas State Historical Society, Topeka)

Left, top: Shortly after the Civil War the 3rd US Artillery Regiment's band came into being, and performed at the Presidio of San Francisco for several years. The men don the jaunty scarlet-trimmed dark blue wool jacket and the distinctive artillery cap with cords and horsetail plume. Their leader appears in the ungainly bearskin, long associated with that position. (Bancroft Library, University of California, Berkeley)

Left, center and bottom: The Union Pacific's *Engine 119* and the Central Pacific's *Jupiter* provide the historic backdrop for the 21st Infantry Regiment's band as they help observe the conclusion of the transcontinental railroad. (Golden Spike National Historic Site)

Right, top: During most of the Victorian era the garrison at Fort Leavenworth, Kansas, enjoyed the diversion of a band such as this one in 1870 from the 5th Infantry Regiment. The men stand before the quarters of the commander, built in the late 1830s for Colonel Stephen Watts Kearny. (Fort Leavenworth Museum)

Right, center: Recalling the Civil War period, a young drummer stands with his older comrades at Fort Rice, North Dakota. The bandsmen are probably those assigned to the 21st Infantry Regiment in the 1870s. (State Historical Society of North Dakota)

Right, bottom: Henry Yeager led the 3rd Infantry Band when this 1872 photograph was taken (possibly at Fort Hays, Kansas). (Old Guard Museum)

OLD FORT RICE N.D. 1864 TO 1880

Left, top: Fort Bridger's 4th Infantry band poses along the banks of the Blacks Fork, early 1870s. The musicians spent over two years at this Wyoming outpost. (Wyoming Archives, Museums and Historical Department)

Left, center: Fourth Artillerymen, led by their band, prepare to parade for the public during Fourth of July celebrations in 1876. The unit's musicians were the featured entertainment in a military extravaganza held in commemoration of the United States' centennial. (Society of California Pioneers)

Left, bottom: During June 1877 photographer F. Jay Haynes preserved the image of the 7th Cavalry's bandsmen. Even after the Little Big Horn they proved a source of morale and *esprit de corps* for the unit. (Haynes Foundation Collection, Montana Historical Society, Helena)

Right, top: These bandsmen, possibly of the 17th Infantry at Fort Yates, North Dakota, in the mid-1870s, provide another example of diversity in the uniform employed from regiment to regiment for the band. Triple rows of buttons, cuffs similar to those used in 1851–54, white cords, white belts and cock feathers are the most significant components of their nonregulation wear. (State Historical Society of North Dakota)

Right, bottom: A Fort Leavenworth bandsman (probably of the 5th Infantry Regiment), again showing variations which existed from the prescribed uniform. The triple row of officer's style buttons, cords, and evidently the use of white facings with scarlet edging would all give the wearer a patriotic and colorful appearance. (Fort Leavenworth Museum)

Left, above: A late 1870s photograph at Whipple Barracks, Arizona Territory, depicting the 8th Infantry Band assembled with both cavalry and infantry troops for a Sunday dress parade. (Sharlot Hall Museum, Prescott, Arizona)

Left, center: Guard mount constituted an important aspect of daily life at each frontier post. Bandsmen, such as these from Fort Assiniboine, Montana, enlivened the ritual. (National Archives)

Above: Supposedly dating from 8 September 1883, this photograph indicates that the 5th Infantry band retained a cap or shako in lieu of the spiked helmet adopted for all foot personnel two years earlier. The musicians are performing as part of the Villard Excursion. (Haynes Foundation Collection, Montana Historical Society, Helena)
Left: By about 1885 the 5th Infantry bandsmen still retained their caps, although they can be contrasted with the several company musicians in their helmets and 1884-pattern regulation coats who appear in the back ranks. Massing the trumpeters and drummers from a company with the band was a typical practice at larger garrisons. (National Archives)

33

Left: Harry Gara, a musician with Company 'I' of the 20th Infantry at Fort Leavenworth, illustrates the uniform coat prescribed for his specialty from 1884 to 1902. He also wears the double stripe on his trouser legs, another regulation aspect for musicians. This uniform was to be worn with the helmet, but Gara opted to appear at the photographer's studio in his forage cap instead. (Fort Leavenworth Museum)

Right, top: Chief Trumpeter John Dineen, of the 6th United States Cavalry, served at Fort Bayard, New Mexico, in the mid-1880s when this photograph was taken. The web belt, lyre buckle, baldric and forage cap are all indicative of his position within the band's organization. (Arizona Historical Society, Tucson)

Far right, top: Musician Wetzell of Fort Bridger, Wyoming, wears his 1884 to 1902-pattern uniform coat with no extra frills. The only means of distinguishing him from a regular infantryman is the presence of 'herringbone' on the chest. (Wyoming State Archives, Museums and Historical Department)

Right, bottom: The 3rd US Cavalry band at Jefferson Barracks, Missouri, in the early 1890s. (National Archives)

Left, top: Another representative variation from regulations was the 'pill box' cap as modelled here by John H. Boyer, Chief Musician of the 15th Infantry, along with gold cord and shoulder knots. (Fort Huachuca Historical Museum)

Above: The grassy parade ground at Fort Keogh, Montana, resounds to the martial tunes of the 5th Infantry in the early 1880s. (National Archives)

Left, center: Herman Trutner Sr. led the 13th Infantry band from Fort Marcy, New Mexico. The bandsmen are assembling here in the plaza of Santa Fe, the territorial capital. (Museum of New Mexico)

Left, bottom: The 9th Cavalry's bandsmen also performed at Santa Fe, providing amusement for the local townsmen as well as helping to break down barriers of racial prejudice. (School of American Research Collections, Museum of New Mexico)

Below: The everyday uniform of the 4th Cavalry band at Fort Huachuca, Arizona, was typical of that issued to all enlisted personnel in the mid-1880s. All the men wear the forage cap and jacket of the era. German names dominate, according to the original identification. (National Archives)

Bottom: The changing composition of the band of the 4th Cavalry in the mid 1880s becomes apparent when comparing this photograph from Fort Bowie, Arizona, with the same organization at Fort Huachuca (previous photo) and Fort Lowell (next photo). (National Archives)

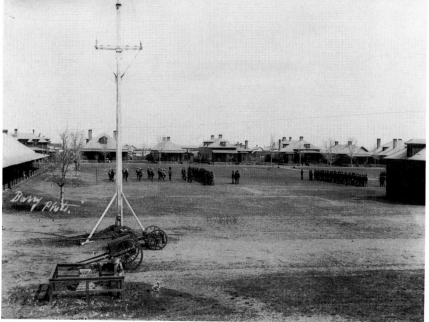

Left, top: The tones of the 1880s 4th Cavalry band no longer echo across the parade ground of Fort Lowell, Arizona, but this photograph and the crumbling remains of the barracks help preserve the memory of this group. (Buehman Collection, Arizona Historical Society, Tucson)

Left, center: The 2nd US Cavalry band and its instruments are clearly evident in this late 1880s or early 1890s informal view. The wreaths and lyres on the forage caps appear to be embroidered. (US Army Military History Institute, Carlisle Barracks, Pennsylvania)

Left, bottom: Noted photographer C. F. Barry found the full dress parade at Fort Yates, North Dakota, an interesting subject in the late 1880s. (Bowen Collection, Custer Battlefield National Monument)

Right, top: In the case of the 3rd Infantry band it appears that the leader (fifth from left) pressed First Sergeant's chevrons into service rather than employing the regulation rank device authorized for his grade. (US Army Military History Institute, Carlisle Barracks, Pennsylvania)

Right, center: In the 23rd Infantry band at Fort Clark, Texas, Germanic names dominated, as seems the pattern. Many foreigners enlisted in the frontier military force and a number of these men joined the bands. (Fort Sam Houston Museum, San Antonio, Texas)

Right, bottom: In 1890 trumpeters from the companies of the 22nd Infantry and 10th Cavalry at Fort Duschene, Utah, formed a makeshift band in response to their relative isolation. The combination of black and white troops was atypical of the segregated practices of the time. (National Archives)

Left, top: The four Black regiments boasted bands of great distinction, as represented here by the members of the 25th Infantry band in their full dress at Fort Randall, South Dakota, in the late 1880s. (South Dakota State Historical Society)

Left, center: White plumes and white breast cords set off the dress garb of the 23rd Infantry in 1886. These men made an invaluable contribution to life at Fort Union, New Mexico. (Fort Sam Houston Museum, San Antonio, Texas)

Left, bottom: By 1887 the 23rd Infantry at Fort Clark, Texas, exhibited all the regalia which evolved from an Army-wide survey of band uniforms of the regiments. The men wear the white shoulder knots with cords and, probably, the new lyre overlay device on their helmet eagles. The use of white helmet cords and the plume proved popular for infantry bands, following the custom (and regulation) for mounted musicians. (Fort Sam Houston Museum, San Antonio, Texas)

Left, top: The 5th Infantry Band performed at the Last Spike Pavilion on 8 September 1883 as one of their many appearances for public occasions. (Haynes Foundation Collection, Montana Historical Society, Helena)

Left, center: Walt Whitman once pronounced the 17th Infantry band the finest he had ever heard. Here members parade through Cheyenne, Wyoming, in the late 1880s for the dedication of the new Capitol building. Appearances of military music groups at civic functions represented a long tradition which helped, to a degree, to forge bonds between townsmen and soldiers. (Wyoming State Archives, Museums and Historical Department)

Below: Fort Reno in today's Oklahoma echoed with the fine music of the 24th Infantry band which appears to the far left of this dress parade formation photograph, *c.* 1887. (National Archives)

Left, top: Mounted officers, followed closely by the band, lead off a typical parade at Fort Logan, Colorado – a ritual repeated all over the frontier on such a regular basis that it became a mainstay of garrison life. (Fort Laramie National Historic Site)

Left, center: Closer inspection of Fort Logan's infantry band reveals that the men have massed the company musicians into their numbers to increase strength for the weekly dress parade. (Fort Laramie National Historic Site)

Below: Captivated by the music, some little girls follow the 'Pied Piper' at Fort D. A. Russell, Wyoming's Sunday parade. Just behind the band, the commanding officer passes on orders to dress up the marching! (Wyoming State Archives, Museums and Historical Department)

Above, top: In the 1890s the 22nd Infantry band donned forage caps in lieu of helmets so that faces would be fully in view for the photograph. The bandsmen wear the regimental number on their belt buckles and, with the exception of the bandmaster to the far left, employ standard enlisted coats rather than musician coats. This seems to have developed as a fairly common practice toward the end of the Victorian era. (National Archives)

Above: Located to the rear of the troops, the 22nd Infantry band (now with their helmets on) provide music for a Fort Keogh, Montana, ceremony. (Montana Historical Society)

Above: The 18th Infantry band plays as the inspecting officer looks over the weapons of the new guard at guard mount, Fort Assiniboine, Montana. In the background, soldiers' bedding hangs on the barracks rails to air. (Montana Historical Society)

Left, center: White summer helmets stand put along with the belts of Fort Niobrara, Nebraska's band as it escorts a funeral procession in the late 1880s. Playing to and from the cemetery was customary. (South Dakota State Historical Society)

Left, bottom: The band at Fort Sam Houston, Texas, dons white summer helmets and trousers for Guard Mount. (Fort Sam Houston Military Museum, San Antonio, Texas)

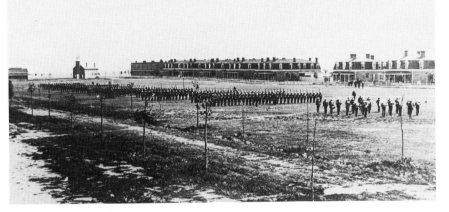

Left, center: Fort Assiniboine, Montana's band joins the entire white-helmeted garrison on the parade ground of the post. Depending on weather and other conditions, formations would be conducted in other than full dress uniform. (National Archives)

Left, bottom: In a rare glimpse of the 'Old Army', Indian Scouts at the right line up with white troops and black troops while the 24th Infantry's regimental band anchors the left end of the line at Fort Reno, Oklahoma. (National Archives)

Left, top: An infantry band accompanies troops and construction workers of the St. Paul, Minneapolis and Manitoba Railway (forerunner of the Great Northern) as the train makes its way toward today's western North Dakota. The picture was taken in 1887, the year the railroad was being extended toward Great Falls and Helena, Montana. (Burlington Northern Railroad)

Left, center: At one time mounted musicians had to be able horsemen as well as capable of playing their instruments. In the upper photo, members of a mounted cavalry band, in full dress and with instruments secured, stand to horse with their mounts. These men are at Douglas, Wyoming, in 1893. Below, the cavalry band at Fort Meade, South Dakota, demonstrates both these talents, *c.* 1890. (Fort Laramie National Historic Site/US Army Military History Institute, Carlisle Barracks, Pennsylvania)

Left, bottom: The band of the 1st Cavalry, in busbies, joins troop buglers in 1898 to put on an impressive show at the US Cavalry School located at Fort Riley, Kansas. (Joseph J. Pennell Collection, Kansas Collection, University of Kansas Libraries)

Right, top: The 2nd Cavalry at Fort Wingate, New Mexico, also favored busbies in lieu of the dress helmet in the 1890s. (US Army Military History Institute, Carlisle Barracks, Pennsylvania)

Right, bottom: The 6th Cavalry band took up duties at Fort Riley near the turn of the century and lent color to the activities at the post. (Joseph J. Pennell Collection, Kansas Collection, University of Kansas Libraries)

Left, top: Paying final tribute to a cavalry comrade in 1895, the Fort Riley band proceeds somberly to the burial grounds. Traditionally, on the return they played a lively tune. (Joseph J. Pennell Collection, Kansas Collection, University of Kansas Libraries)

Left, center: Though seen here in the 1890s, the 11th Infantry band at this guard mount could have been anywhere at a frontier post in the decades following the Civil War since the ceremony constituted a basic element of military life in the West. (US Army Military History Institute, Carlisle Barracks, Pennsylvania)

Left, bottom and below: Not all band activities took place on the parade ground, nor at the main post, as is evident by these two views of the Fort Robinson (8th Infantry) band in the late Victorian era, with musicians accompanying their comrades to a training camp for field instruction and practice (Don Rickey Jr. Collection)

Right, top: A rather ragtag group of trumpeters assembles in the field at Fort Riley in 1897. These men sometimes enjoyed more prestige when they temporarily took their places alongside the regimental band for ceremonies. (Joseph J. Pennell Collection, Kansas Collection, University of Kansas Libraries)

Far right, top: Private Thomas of the 4th Cavalry band's campaign hat displays the lyre and wreath insignia, marking him as a musician in this 1901 photograph. (Joseph J. Pennell Collection, Kansas Collection, University of Kansas Libraries)

Right, center: Weather conditions did not dissuade the military from carrying on with its routine: Fort Riley's bandsmen in 1901 simply brought out their greatcoats with capes for guard mount on a brisk day. (Joseph J. Pennell Collection, Kansas Collection, University of Kansas Libraries)

Right, bottom: A trio of bandsmen relax on the barracks porch at Fort Riley, Kansas, in 1898. In addition to their musical duties the men had regular chores such as wood-cutting details and daily stable call. (Joseph J. Pennell Collection, Kansas Collection, University of Kansas Libraries)

Far right, bottom: C. E. Bordon served as an infantry trombonist at Fort Lyon, Colorado, when this studio photograph was taken. (Kansas State Historical Society, Topeka)

Far left, top: Trombonist John McCauley wore a lyre on his belt plate, as did many other bandsmen during the 1880s through the turn of the century. He served with Fort Riley's cavalry band in 1900. (Joseph J. Pennell Collection, Kansas Collection, University of Kansas Libraries)

Left, top: In this portrait of 6th Cavalry bandsmen George L. Brown the gold cord is absent and all other items of wear are strictly 'by the book.' (Joseph J. Pennell Collection, Kansas Collection, University of Kansas Libraries)

Far left, bottom: Sergeant Roach, bandmaster for the 6th Cavalry in 1898, wears a triple-breasted platron front and officer's style shoulder knots with crossed baton devices as part of his distinctive garb. He has replaced his dress headgear with a forage cap for this portrait. (Joseph J. Pennell Collection, Kansas Collection, University of Kansas Libraries)

Left, bottom: Sergeant Blake of the 4th Cavalry band in 1901 wore an officer's jacket with his dark yellow chevrons and a lyre on each side of the collar for his undress uniform while posing with a friend for this portrait. A number of civilian bands adopted similar garb during this era. (Joseph J. Pennell Collection, Kansas Collection, University of Kansas Libraries)

Above: Enjoying a holiday meal, the 23rd Infantry band breaks from its military music routine. In many instances these men served together for an extended period of time and developed a close relationship as a unit as well as considerable skill as a band. (Fort Sam Houston Military Museum, San Antonio, Texas)

Left: In the 1890s Fort Sam Houston's band called this building 'home'. The musicians at all posts shared a barracks which was often smaller than that provided for the companies, troops and batteries due to the relatively few men who made up the musical complement. In some instances these structures were also built away from the main parade ground so that practice sessions would not disturb the rest of the post. (Fort Sam Houston Military Museum, San Antonio, Texas)

Left, top: Philip Schreiper of Company 'H', 18th US Infantry, appears here in his forage cap instead of the proper dress helmet prescribed for the uniform coat he wears. Such variations were common for musicians serving in bands, although Schreiper probably took this liberty for the sake of the portrait photographer. (Fort Leavenworth Museum)

Left, bottom: Band instruments of the 1st Cavalry at Fort Riley, along with music stands and carrying cases, were maintained in an orderly fashion. For decades after the Civil War the government provided no funds to purchase these tools of the trade, thus money generated from the company and regimental fund as well as from subscriptions and private donations was required in order to purchase these expensive items. (Joseph J. Pennell Collection, Kansas Collection, University of Kansas Libraries)

APPENDICES

APPENDIX 1: THE MUSIC

No study of the history of bands can be complete without an examination of the music commonly played in that period. This music showed clearly the tastes of the populace, and although it is only a small part, it is nevertheless an important part of the cultural heritage. Band music of the second half of the nineteenth century generally exhibited simplicity of melodic line and accompaniment. Harmonic analysis shows that the principal chordal features have a tonic-subdominant-dominant-tonic relationship.[1] Types of music were varied. The primary kinds were marches, dance tunes, popular songs, religious songs and hymns, and an occasional orchestral transcription. There were usually pieces which could easily be arranged for various instrumental combinations.

Several excellent recordings of recreated bands have been made since 1960. These, along with some programs of concerts by regimental bands, were the primary sources for studying music performed during the period 1866–91. A few journal articles do furnish additional information, but unfortunately too little research has been done in this area.

To facilitate this study the following categories were devised, and all of the numbers available for examination were then placed with them: 1. Patriotic tunes; 2. Marches and quicksteps; 3. Popular songs; 4. Religious songs; 5. Dance tunes; 6. Orchestral and classical transcriptions; 7. Miscellaneous. Sources consulted included recordings of music of the Civil War and post-Civil War eras, programs of concerts by various regimental bands, a catalogue of the works of composer John Philip Sousa, and microfilm of various band books of the period.[2]

PATRIOTIC TUNES

The Battle Hymn of the Republic	Steffe
The Fourth of July Overture	arr. 'Mixture'
Hail! Columbia	Phile
Hail to the Chief	arr. Sanderson
The Marseilles [sic]	Unknown
Maryland, My Maryland	Unknown
The Star Spangled Banner	arr. Dodworth
We Are Coming, Father Abraham	Emerson
Yankee Doodle	Unknown

MARCHES AND QUICKSTEPS

Adjutant Smithers March	Ferrazi
Amathusia Quickstep	Kalkman
American Exposition March	Beyer
Annie May Quickstep	arr. Friederich
Blues Quickstep	Unknown
Brightest Eyes Quickstep	Gilmore
Cavalry Quickstep	Grafulla
Celestial Grand March	Lange
Cheer, Boys, Cheer	Russell
Col. White's Quickstep	Grafulla
Congo's Quickstep	Unknown
Der Alpin Jaeger [sic] *March*	Beyer
Eaton's Grand March	Eaton
8th Regiment M.V.M. Quickstep	Reeves
Ellen Bayne Quickstep	arr. Friederich
Farewell, My Lilly Dear	arr. Friederich
La Fille du Tambour Major	Offenbach
Free and Easy Quickstep	arr. Downing
The Gladiator	Sousa
Grand March No. 8	Grafulla
Irish Medley Quickstep	Unknown
Italian Prize Quickstep	Arditti
Lilly Bell Quickstep	arr. Friederich
Luto Quickstep	Unknown
Mandolita March	Unknown
Massa's in the Cold Ground	arr. Friederich

My Old Kentucky Home	arr. Friederich
Ocean Tide March	arr. Friederich
Old Dog Tray	arr. Friederich
The Old Log Hut	arr. Friederich
Our Flirtations	Sousa
Peter's Quickstep	Unknown
Quickstep	W. Held
Quickstep Medley	arr. Grafulla
Resumption	Sousa
Semper Fidelis	Sousa
Seventh Cavalry Quickstep	arr. W. Held
Signal March	arr. Friederich
10th US Cavalry March	Brenner
Turkish Reveille	Goetz
Washington Post	Sousa
The Young Recruit Medley	Scala

POPULAR SONGS

The Bonnie Blue Flag	McCarthy
Come, Dearest,	
The Daylight is Gone	Unknown
Come Where my Love Lies Dreaming	Foster
Dixie	Emmett
Eileen Allana	Thomas
Garry Owen	Unknown
The Girl I Left Behind Me	Unknown
Goober Peas	Blackmar
Happy Moments	arr. Bracht
Kathleen Mavoureen	arr. Bracht
Listen to the	
Mocking Bird	Septimus Winner[3]
Lulu's Gone	Foster
Maggie By My Side	arr. Friederich
Marching Through Georgia	Work
Old Kentucky, Kentucky	Unknown
Song – My Own Guiding Star	'Robin Hood'
Thou Art So Near	
and Yet So Far	arr. Bracht
Tenting on the Old Camp Ground	Kittridge
Tramp, Tramp, Tramp	Root
When Johnny Comes	
Marching Home	Louis Lambert[4]

RELIGIOUS SONGS

Alma Redemtoris	Unknown
Austrian Hymn	Haydn
Cujus Amenene	Rossini
May Heaven's Graces	Unknown
Nearer, My God to Thee	Lowell Mason
Old Hundredth	Genevan Psalter
Sweet Spirit, Hear My Prayer	Unknown

DANCE TUNES

Andante and Waltz No. 39	Grafulla
Ashuelot Waltzes	Howard
Bird of Paradise Waltz	Ingals
Bird Polka	P. Held
Blitz Galop	Faust
Camp May Polka	Grafulla
Dash Away Galop	Barthman

Doctrine Waltz	Strauss
Easter Galop	Unknown
Enclume Polka	Barlow
En Evant Galop	arr. W. Held
Ever Feliz Mazourka	Nieva
La Fille de Mad-Ingot	
Quadrille	arr. P. Held
Fireman's Polka	Unknown
For Ever Thine Gavotte	Weiss
Galop	Mueller
Genl. McLaughlin's Schottische	Brenner
Immortellon Waltz	Gung'l
Infernal Galop	Keter Bela
Jewel Waltz	Friederich
Jullien's Rosita –	
Valse Espagnole	arr. Metra
Waltz Knaebel	Unknown
Laughing Beauty Galop	Keller
Les Rendezvous Waltzes	Unknown
Luna Polka	Peplow
Museum Waltz	J. Catlin
Nathalie Waltz	arr. P. Held
Neptune Galop	Unknown
Nightingale Waltz	Grafulla
On the Beautiful Rhine Waltz	Keter Bela
Palmyra Schottische	Grafulla
Parting Waltz	Weisenberg
Pelham Schottische	Friederich
Rainbow Schottische	Friederich
Rendezvous Galop	C. Faust
San Antonio Waltzes	Gung'l
Soldaten Lieder Waltz	arr. Held
Storm Galop	Grafulla
Tanz Berlin Waltz	Gung'l
Un Suspiro Parati (Danza)	Nieva
Venus Waltz	Grafulla
Waltz	Grafulla
Wedding Schottische	Friederich

ORCHESTRAL AND CLASSICAL TRANSCRIPTIONS

Bohemian Girl (Grand Selection)	Balfe
Ernani (Selection)	Verdi
Freischutz Quickstep	Weber
Fatinitza (Selection)	Suppé
HMS Pinafore (Grand Potpourri)	Sullivan
Light Cavalry (Overture)	Suppé
Macbeth (Potpourri)	Verdi
Martha (Selections)	Flotow
Nabucco (Overture)	Verdi
Norma (Introduction)	Bellini
Puritani (Potpourri)	Bellini
Stabat Mater (Selections)	Rossini
La Traviata (Grand Fantasy)	Verdi
Trial By Jury (Selection)	Sullivan
William Tell (Grand Selection)	Rossini

MISCELLANEOUS

American Medley	Benedict
Il Baccio	arr. Bracht

Call Me Not Back		
from the Endless Shore		Grafulla
Capriccio		rearr. Held
Le Cheval de Bronze Overture		arr. P. Held
Crown of Gold Overture		Hermann
Departed Days Serenade		Unknown

APPENDIX II: INSTRUMENTATION

Instrumentation means the distribution of parts of a composition among the members of a musical organization. While composers and music publishers generally specify a certain instrumentation for a composition, in many cases this serves only as a general guideline because some instruments may not be available or more of others than desired are available. In addition, no two publishers ever agree upon a standard instrumentation. The result is, and always has been, a hodge-podge of instrumentations and groups of various sizes and varying instrumentations.

Two publications which suggested intrumentations for military bands during the nineteenth century were the *Brass Band School* and *The Brass Band Journal*.[1] Both were combined instruction and concert books and although both were designed primarily for use by brass bands, woodwinds could be substituted for some of the parts. The instrumentations from each are listed, side by side for purposes of comparison, in Table 2.

The only difference between these two books was that the *Brass Band School* had two trombone parts which were not present in *The Brass Band Journal*. An examination of several of the compositions included in the

Brass Band School showed that in some cases the baritone and trombone parts were similar and in other cases totally different; furthermore, in the preface to the book, Allen Dodworth stated that he would prefer not to include trombone parts, but that the public demanded it.[2]

Only three bands of the period were located in which the instrumentation was specified; these are listed, side by side for purposes of comparison, in Table 3. As may be seen, all three bands had certain instruments in common, *viz.* E♭ cornet; B♭ cornet (generally four parts); alto (at least three parts); trombone (at least two each); baritone; E♭ tuba (two each); snare drum; and bass drum. When compared to the suggested instrumentations given in the *Brass Band School* and *The Brass Band Journal*, it was found that, with one exception, the recommended instrumentations were complied with. The exception may be explained by the fact that by 1876 (and

TABLE 2
SUGGESTED INSTRUMENTATIONS
FOR MILITARY BANDS

Brass Band School	Brass Band Journal
E♭ soprano (first)	E♭ soprano (first)
E♭ soprano (second)	E♭ soprano (second)
B♭ alto (first)	B♭ alto (first)
B♭ alto (second)	B♭ alto (second)
E♭ tenor (first)	E♭ tenor (first)
E♭ tenor (second)	E♭ tenor (second)
Baritone	Baritone
Bass (first)	Basso (first)
Bass (second)	Basso (second)
E♭ trumpet	E♭ trumpet
Trombone (first)	
Trombone (second)	
Snare drum	Small drum
Bass drum	Bass drum

TABLE 3
INSTRUMENTATIONS FOR SPECIFIED
MILITARY BANDS

2nd Cavalry, 1876[4]	6th Cavalry, 1894[5]	18th Infantry, 1886[6]
Piccolo		
E♭ clarinet		E♭ clarinet
B♭ clarinet		B♭ clarinet
B♭ clarinet		B♭ clarinet
B♭ clarinet		B♭ clarinet
B♭ clarinet		B♭ clarinet
B♭ clarinet		
E♭ cornet	E♭ cornet	E♭ cornet
B♭ cornet	Cornet (solo)	B♭ cornet (solo)
B♭ cornet	Cornet (first)	B♭ cornet
B♭ cornet	Cornet (second)	B♭ cornet
	Cornet (third)	B♭ cornet
E♭ trumpet		
E♭ saxhorn		
Alto	Alto (first)	Alto (solo)
Alto	Alto (second)	Alto (first)
Alto		
Trombone	Trombone (first)	Tenor (first)[7]
Trombone	Trombone (second)	Tenor (second)[7]
Baritone	Baritone	Baritone
Euphonium		
	B♭ Tuba	
Tuba	E♭ Tuba	E♭ tuba
Tuba	E♭ Tuba	E♭ tuba
Snare Drum	Snare Drum	
		Tenor drum[8]
Bass Drum	Bass Drum	Bass drum
Cymbals	Cymbals	

55

thereafter) B♭ cornets had taken the place of E♭ cornets. It should be noted that in some cases there were more of certain parts than recommended in the books, but the recommended numbers were present. In no case was there less than the recommended number of instruments in any of the bands.[3]

The addition of woodwinds by two of the bands was probably a matter of taste as these were not prerequisites for a band of the period. However, to effectively play orchestral transcriptions, woodwinds were necessary to render string parts with the smoothness and mellowness which one would hear in the original version. The mounted band (6th Cavalry) obviously could not use woodwinds owing to the simple fact that both hands are vital in playing woodwinds whereas brass instruments may be easily managed with one hand.

NOTES

INTRODUCTION

1. Charles King, *The Colonel's Daughter or Winning His Spurs* (Philadelphia: J. B. Lippincott Co., 1895), p. 26. Such an episode is not improbable since the Fort Lyon, Colorado, garrison gave a *masque* in 1873 which was attended by individuals from Forts Dodge, Leavenworth, Riley and Wallace. 'The orchestra consisted of six musicians from the regimental band at Fort Riley.' Frances M. A. Roe, *Army Letters from an Officer's Wife* (Lincoln: University of Nebraska Press, 1981), p. 144.

2. King, a medically retired cavalry officer, was noted for his accuracy since he drew many of his early stories from personal journals. Oliver Knight, *Life and Manners in the Frontier Army* (Norman: University of Oklahoma Press, 1978), makes a convincing case for King's dependability as a source for social history.

3. King, *The Colonel's Daughter*, p. 42. Alice Blackwood Baldwin, *Memoirs of the Late Frank D. Baldwin, Major General, USA* (Los Angeles: Wetzel Publishing Co., 1924), p. 14, describes the lengths to which the 5th Infantry went when organizing one of their dances. Other memoirs tend to substantiate King's claim.

4. John P. Gates, 'The Alleged Isolation of US Army Officers in the Late 19th Century,' *Parameters*, X (September 1980), pp. 32–45, contends that the civilian and military populations in the West made frequent contacts rather than remaining separate entities. This argument is greatly reinforced as regards the role of military bands.

5. Donald J. Mrozek, 'The Army and Popular Culture,' in Robin Higham and Carol Brandt (eds.), *The United States Army in Peacetime: Essays in Honor of the Bicentennial, 1775–1975* (Manhattan, Kansas: Military Affairs/ Aerospace Historian Publishing, 1975), p. 141, mentions this concept in passing.

6. Fairfax Downey devoted a few chapters on the subject in his *Fyfe, Drum & Bugle* (Fort Collins, Colorado: The Old Army Press, 1971). John S. Buchanan's 'Functions of the Fort Davis Military Bands and Musical Proclivities of the Commanding Officer, Colonel Benjamin H. Grierson, Late Nineteenth Century' (unpublished Master's thesis, Sul Ross State College, 1968) offers insight into one western military post's band. William Carter White's *A History of Military Music in America* (New York: Greenwood Press, 1975) should be consulted for earlier periods, as should Allen J. Ferguson, 'Trumpets, Bugles and Horns in North America, 1750–1815,' *Military Collector and Historian*, XXXVI (Spring 1984), pp. 2–7, and Ferguson's 'The Military Music Scene in Plattsburgh, NY: Fifes, Drums and Bands in 1814–1819,' *Military Collector and Historian*, XXXV (Fall 1983), p. 112. Two more recent articles in *Military Collector and Historian* are likewise noteworthy. They are Larry L. Nelson, 'Two Military Bands on the Northwest Frontier During the War of 1812,' XXXVI (Summer 1984), pp. 67–9 and David Simmons, 'The Band of Music in the American Army of 1787,' XXXVII (Fall 1985), pp. 135–6.

CHAPTER I

1. Simon V. Anderson, 'The Unofficial Bands of the American Revolution,' *Music Educators Journal*, LXI (December 1974), pp. 26–8.

2. John C. Fitzpatrick, 'The Bands of the Continental Army,' *Daughters of the American Revolution Magazine*, LVII (April 1923), pp. 187–97 *passim*. Although this article purports to deal with bands, it is actually concerned with fife and drum corps. Fitzpatrick believed that bands and fife and drum corps were one and the same. No information on bands prior to the revolution was located.

3. Oscar G. Sonneck, *Early Concert Life in America* (Wiesbaden, Germany: Dr Martin Sandig oHG., 1969), pp. 318–19.

4. George P. Carroll, 'The Band of Musick of the Second Virginia Regiment,' *Journal of Band Research*, II (n.d.), p. 16.

5. *Ibid.*

6. Fitzpatrick, 'Bands of the Continental Army,' pp. 187–8, 190–1.

7. Anderson, 'Unofficial Bands,' pp. 29–30.

8. *Ibid.*, p. 30.

9. *Ibid.*, pp. 30–3 *passim*.

10. Camus, 'The Military Band Prior to 1834,' pp. 420–4 *passim*.

11. *Ibid.*, pp. 426–30 *passim*.

12. *Ibid.*, pp. 434–47 *passim*.

13. *Ibid.*, pp. 476–8.

14. *Ibid.*, p. 481; also p. 475. Sutlers were traders licensed to sell articles to troops stationed at military posts.

15. *Ibid.*, p. 488.

16. *Ibid.*, p. 490.

17. White, *Military Music in America*, pp. 38–9.

18. On 10 December 1858 the St. Louis *Daily Missouri*

Republican noted that four regimental bands participated in military ceremonies held at Camp Floyd, Utah. This gathering was an unusual one since such a concentration of troops did not take place on a regular basis in the West prior to the Civil War, or after it for that matter.

19. Francis Paul Prucha, *Broadax and Bayonet: The Role of the United States Army in the Development of the Northwest, 1815–1860* (Lincoln: University of Nebraska Press, 1967), p. 203.

20. Charles P. Roland and Richard Robbins (eds.), 'The Diary of Eliza (Mrs. Albert Sidney) Johnston,' *Southwestern Historical Quarterly*, LX (April 1957), p. 484.

CHAPTER II

1. Francis A. Lord and Arthur Wise, *Bands and Drummer Boys of the Civil War* (New York: Thomas Yoseloff, 1966), p. 28.

2. *Ibid.*, pp. 16, 20; Bufkin, 'Union Bands,' p. 34. Patrick S. Gilmore was an Irish emigrant who settled in the United States in 1848. He was acknowledged as the greatest cornet soloist of his day. His first position as a band director was with the Salem, Massachusetts Brass Band. From there, he went to Boston where he directed the Boston Brigade Band. This band enlisted with the 24th Massachusetts Infantry and served until August 1862, when it was discharged. After the war Gilmore became the leading bandmaster in the United States, a position which he held until his death in September 1892, the month in which John Philip Sousa began his career as a civilian bandmaster. No information concerning C. S. Grafulla or Joseph Green has been located.

3. US *Congressional Globe, Containing the Debates and Proceedings, 1833–1873* (190 vols.; Washington: Blair and Rives, *et al.*, editors and publishers, 1834–1873), 29 July 1861, I, 37th Cong., 1st sess., App. pp. 29–30.

4. US War Department, *War of the Rebellion: A Compilation of Official Records of the Union and Confederate Armies* (128 vols.; Washington: Government Printing Office, 1880–1891), 3rd series, I, pp. 372–3. Hereafter cited as *O.R.*

5. *Ibid.*

6. *Ibid.*

7. *Ibid.*

8. *Ibid.*

9. US Congress, House, House Executive Document No. 72, *Regimental Bands*, 37th Cong., 2nd sess., 1862 (microcard), Serial No. 1131, pp. 1–4. Herafter cited as *Regimental Bands*.

10. *Congressional Globe*, 4 February 1862, II, 37th Cong., 2nd sess., p. 593.

11. *Regimental Bands*.

12. *Ibid.*

13. *Ibid.*

14. *O.R.*, 3rd series, I, p. 381.

15. Lord and Wise, *Bands and Drummer Boys*, pp. 53–5.

16. *O.R.*, 3rd series, II, p. 278.

17. *Ibid.*

18. Bell I. Wiley, *The Life of Billy Yank: The Common Soldier of the Union* (Garden City, N.Y.: Doubleday and Co., 1971), p. 158.

19. *Ibid.*

20. *Ibid.*

21. Lord and Wise, *Bands and Drummer Boys*, p. 48.

22. *Ibid.*, pp. 177–8.

23. *Ibid.*, p. 178.

24. *Ibid.*, p. 187.

25. *Ibid.*

26. *Ibid.*, p. 193.

27. *Ibid.*, pp. 199–200.

28. *Ibid.*, pp. 171–6 *passim*.

29. *Ibid.*

30. *Ibid.*, p. 181.

31. *Ibid.*, pp. 181–3.

32. *Ibid.*, pp. 178–81.

33. Additional information concerning this period is contained in Robert Garofalo and Mark Elrod, *A Pictorial History of Civil War Era Musical Instruments and Military Bands* (Charleston, West Virginia: Pictorial Histories Publishing Co., 1985) and Kenneth E. Olson, *Music and Musket: Bands and Bandsmen of the American Civil War* (Westport, Connecticut: Greenwood Press, 1981).

CHAPTER III

1. Elizabeth B. Custer, *Following the Guidon* (Norman: University of Oklahoma Press, 1966), p. xxix.

2. Lt. Charles Delano Hine, 'Uniform,' *The United Service: A Monthly Review of Military and Naval Affairs* (May 1895), p. 410.

3. Organizational Returns, Tenth Cavalry, July–October 1867, Circular, B. Grierson to Company Commanders, 14 September 1867, Letters Sent, Tenth Cavalry as quoted in William H. Leckie, *The Buffalo Soldiers: A Narrative of the Negro Cavalry in the West* (Norman: University of Oklahoma Press, 1967), p. 17.

4. John M. Carroll, 'The Seventh Cavalry's Band,' *Little Big Horn Associates' Research Review*, IX (Spring 1975), pp. 16–18.

5. US War Department, *Revised Army Regulations, 1873* House Report No. 85, 42nd Cong. 3rd sess., I, 1874 (Serial 1576), p. 19.

6. Colonel De Lancey Floyd-Jones to Assistant Adjutant General William W. Whipple, 5 September 1872, Letters Sent, Fort Hays, Kansas, Records of US Army Commands, record Group 393, National Archives and Records Service (Microfilm), hereafter cited as RUSAC, RG 393, NARS. Supposedly, Colonel Floyd-Jones was extremely fond of his band to the degree that he 'babied the bandsmen, one and all, until they had quite forgotten the fact of their being enlisted men.' As a consequence they once refused to perform a fatigue detail until the clever regimental adjutant persuaded them to change their mind. Frances M. A. Roe, *Army Letters from an Officer's Wife* (Lincoln: University of Nebraska Press, 1981), p. 355.

7. Francis B. Heitman, *Historical Register and Dictionary of the United States Army, 1789 to 1902*, 2 vols. (Washington, DC: Government Printing Office, 1903), II, p. 604.

8. Letter, Robert Greenhalgh to Parents, Fort Laramie, Dakota Territory, 7 December 1866; typescript copy furnished by Dr. Don Rickey Jr.

9. *Annual Report of the Secretary of War, 1875*, House Executive Doc. No. 1, pt. II, 44th Cong., 2nd sess., Vol. I, 1876 (Serial 1674), p. 4.

10. *Congressional Globe*, 40th Cong., 3rd sess., 3 March 1869, Appendix, pp. 318–19.

11. Secretary of War to Speaker of the House, *Regimental Bands for the Army*, 9 July 1890, House Ex. Doc. No. 446, 51st Cong., 1st sess., XXXVII, 1891 (Serial 2752).

12. *Ibid.*

13. Leckie, *The Buffalo Soldiers*, p. 17.

14. Alfred Gibbs to Myles Keogh, 28 April 1867, Letters Sent, Headquarters, Smoky Hill District, Smoky Hill Subdistrict Papers, RUSAC, RG 393, NARS.

15. Carroll, 'The Seventh Cavalry's Band,' pp. 16–17.

16. *Ibid.*

17. George Crook to Jefferson C. Davis, 3 May 1872, George Crook Papers, US Army Military History Research Collection, Carlisle Barracks, Pennsylvania. *Regulations* *for the Army of the United States, 1889* called for 'suitable men' to be enlisted for bands.

18. Fairfax Downey, *Indian Fighting Army* (New York: Charles Scribner's Sons, 1941), p. 24. According to Baldwin, *Memoirs*, p. 14, the 5th US Infantry band was composed mainly of foreigners, principally Italians. Their leader 'Giovanni,' who later achieved some fame with the US Marine Corps Band in Washington, DC.

19. Martha Summerhayes, *Vanished Arizona: Recollections of My Army Life* (Chicago: The Lakeside Press, 1939), p. 15.

20. Downey, *Fyfe, Drum and Bugle*, pp. 123–30.

21. New York *Times*, 21 September 1947, p. 34.

22. Anthony Powell, 'Keep Step to the Music of the Union: A History of Black Regular Army Bands, 1869–1930' (unpublished manuscript, San Jose, California, 1980), p. 9.

23. *Ibid.*, p. 5.

24. *Ibid.*, p. 9.

25. Harry Carr's *Arizona Lancer* as quoted in *ibid.*, pp. 9–10.

26. *Revised United States Army Regulations of 1861 with an Appendix Containing Changes and Laws Affecting Army Regulations and Articles of War to June 25, 1863* (Washington, DC: Government Printing Office, 1863), p. 481.

27. For a comparison with the regular dress of the day see J. Phillip Langellier, *They Continually Wear the Blue: US Army Enlisted Dress Uniforms, 1865–1902* (San Francisco: Barnes-McGee, 1976).

28. George L. Andrews to Assistant Adjutant General, Department of Texas, 4 October 1875, Letters Sent, Fort Davis, Texas, RUSAC, RG 393, NARS.

29. Summerhayes, *Vanished Arizona*, p. 299.

30. Thomas J. Carpenter and Rheda Fry, *Old West Army Cookbook, 1865–1900* (Santa Fe: Museum of New Mexico, 1974) discusses the ration.

31. Organizational Returns, 6th Cavalry, February 1871, Records of the Adjutant General's Office, RG 94, NARS.

32. Junction City (Kansas) *Union*, 4 April 1874.

33. James T. King, *War Eagle: A Life of General Eugene A. Carr* (Lincoln: University of Nebraska Press, 1963), p. 103.

34. Robert Carriker, *Fort Supply, Indian Territory: Frontier Outpost on the Plains* (Norman: University of Oklahoma Press, 1970), p. 153; Edgar I. Stewart, *Custer's Luck* (Norman: University of Oklahoma Press, 1955), p. 164.

35. Robert M. Utley, *The Last Days of the Sioux Nation* (New Haven: Yale University Press, 1963), p. 269.

36. Emory Upton, *Infantry Tactics, Double and Single Rank: Adapted to American Topography and Improved Fire-Arms* (New York: Greenwood Press, 1968), pp. 347–8.

37. Jack D. Foner, *The United States Army Between Two Wars: Army Life and Reforms, 1865–1891* (New York: Humanities Press, 1970), p. 90.

38. *Revised Regulations, 1873*, p. 20.

39. Carriker, *Fort Supply*, p. 153.

40. General W. E. Strong, *A Trip to the Yellowstone National Park in July, August and September, 1875* (Norman: University of Oklahoma Press, 1968), p. 8.

41. *Ibid.*, pp. 13–14.

42. Billings *Herald*, 8 September 1883.

43. Helena *Daily Herald*, 10 September 1883.

44. 'Grand Opening Concert' Program, 8 September 1883, Vertical File, Montana Historical Society.

45. Lawrence (Kansas) *Daily Republican*, 15 June 1876.

46. *The Yellowstone Journal*, 12 April 1890.

47. William Warren Rucker, *The Grand Duke Alexis in the United States of America* (New York: Interland Press, 1971), p. 159.

48. *Ibid.*, p. 190.

49. Arlen W. Fowler, *The Black Infantry in the West, 1865–1891* (Westport, Connecticut: Negro Universities Press, 1971), p. 64.

50. Summerhayes, *Vanished Arizona*, pp. 36–7. King, *The Colonel's Daughter*, pp. 369–71, describes a similar military funeral.

51. Elizabeth B. Custer, *Boots and Saddles: or Life in Dakota with General Custer* (Norman: University of Oklahoma Press, 1961), pp. 217–18.

52. Foner, *US Soldier*, p. 90.

53. *Ibid.*

54. Denver (Colorado) *Rocky Mountain News*, 28 September 1872; scrapbook of 1st Lt. Fayette W. Roe, 3rd US Infantry, microfilm copy in Montana Historical Society Archives, Helena, Montana.

55. Musicians Protection Union to Commander, 1st Artillery, 17 July 1888, Letters Received, Presidio of San Francisco, California, RUSAC, RG 393, NARS. A 21 July 1885 decision of the Secretary of War granted permission to Army bands to play at engagements for parties and other functions outside of the military, provided that the prices charged were not lower than the rates charged by civilians who offered similar services locally. A decade later a bill was drafted 'in the interest of citizen musicians in their desire to prohibit competition of military bands.' *Annual Report of the Secretary of War, 1896* (Washington, DC: Government Printing Office, 1896), p. 196.

56. Charles S. King, *Campaigning with Crook* (Norman: University of Oklahoma Press, 1964), p. 4. During the next decade another observer noted that the 3rd Infantry's band was 'out guard mounting every pleasant morning,' and 'each Friday evening' they held a fine concert followed by 'a little dance.' Roe, *Army Letters*. p. 214.

57. Louis Untermeyer (ed.), *The Poetry and Prose of Walt Whitman* (New York: Simon and Schuster, 1949), p. 372. Another indication of how pleased local civilians were with Army bands can be found in a performance given by the 3rd Infantry's musicians in 1878. Montanans and military personnel alike found one particular ball 'most enjoyable, and it was simply enchanting to dance once more to the perfect music of the dear old orchestra. And young people in Helena are showing their appreciation of the good music by dancing themselves positively thin this winter. The band leader brought from New Orleans the Creole music which was so popular there, and at the ball we danced *Varieties* four times; . . . It is thoroughly French, bringing the waltz, polka, schotische, mazurka and redowa.' Roe, *Army Letters*, p. 185.

58. Merrill J. Mattes (ed.), *Indians, Infants and Infantry: Andrew and Elizabeth Burt on the Frontier* (Denver, Colorado: The Old West Publishing Company, 1960), p. 264.

APPENDIX I

1. Tonic, subdominant, and dominant refer to chords constructed upon the first, fourth, and fifth tones of a scale.

2. Although most of Sousa's composing dates from a period later than that under consideration, a few of his compositions were written before 1891 and are thus worthy of inclusion in this study. Of his better-known works, only the ones in this study were written before 1891; 'The Stars and Stripes Forever,' Sousa's best-known opus, was not written until 1896. The lists of music contained in Appendix I were compiled from the following sources: *The Army in the West, Military Music in America*, Vol. III, (Providence: Company of Military Historians, n.d.); 'The Union Army Band,' *Military Music in America*, Vol. IV, (Providence: Company of Military Historians, 1969);

'Ruffles and Flourishes,' Eastman Wind Ensemble, Frederick Fennell, Conductor (Rochester: Eastman School of Music), Mercury Records SRI 78034; 'Music of the Civil War,' Eastman Wind Ensemble, Fennell (Rochester: Eastman School of Music), Mercury Records SRI 2-77011; 'The Spirit of '76,' Eastman Wind Ensemble, Fennell (Rochester: Eastman School of Music), Mercury Records SRI 75048; 'Homespun America,' Eastman Wind Ensemble, Donald Hunsberger, Conductor (Rochester: Eastman School of Music, 1976), Vox SVBX 5309; Paul E. Bierly, *John Philip Sousa: A Descriptive Catalog of His Works* (Urbana: University of Illinois Press, 1973); The Graff Collection, The Newberry Library, Chicago, Nos. 4279–4284; programs contained in various newspapers of the era.

3. 'Septimus Winner' was a pseudonym for Alice Hawthorne, a popular female composer of the mid-nineteenth century.

4. 'Louis Lambert' was a pseudonym for Patrick Gilmore, a bandmaster whose career undoubtedly influenced John Philip Sousa.

APPENDIX II

1. Allen Dodworth, *Brass Band School* (New York: H. B. Dodworth and Co., 1853), and G. W. E. Friederich (arr.), *The Brass Band Journal* (New York: Firth, Pond and Co., 1853).

2. Dodworth, *Brass Band School*, p. 7.

3. According to 1st Lt. W. W. Gulbraith, May 1896, Letters Received, Presidio of San Francisco, California, RUSAC, RG 393, NARS, a partial list of instruments for the band at that post included three altos, one baritone, three bassos, five clarinets, six cornets, two flutes, and three trombones. These figures and the various photographs which appear throughout this publication indicate that the military bands in the West attempted to follow the instrumentation set down in works such as the *Brass Band School* and *The Brass Band Journal*. The same statement may be made to a certain degree when comparing these works with *Regulations for the United States Army, 1895* (Washington: Government Printing Office, 1895), p. 168, which prescribed the following instruments to be furnished by the Quartermaster Department for Army bands: D♭ piccolo, terz and concert flutes, E♭ and B♭ cornets, E♭ trumpets, E♭ and B♭ clarinets, E♭ altos, B♭ trombone (slide or valve), B♭ baritones, E♭ and B♭ bassos, bass and snare drums, cymbals and triangles. Bands were also to receive spare parts for repair and music stands. Mounted bands could substitute a pair of kettledrums in lieu of the bass and snare, cymbals and triangles. They could also be issued with altos, trombones, and bassos of helicon shape. Each light battery of artillery was to receive two small B♭ bugles and all companies were to have two G trumpets with F slides, and, if desired, F crooks. Foot troops could substitute a fife and a drum for the trumpets if the regimental commander desired this exchange. In that same year, *The Annual Report of the Secretary of War, 1895* (Washington: US Government Printing Office, 1895), p. 272, noted that there was some dissatisfaction over the band instruments procured for a number of reasons. As a consequence, the War Department decided to allow greater latitude for bands to select their instruments based upon the standard. Also, cavalry regiments had in certain instances been 'supplied with helicon-shaped instruments,' and the results were supposedly satisfactory.

4. Laramie (Wyoming) *Daily Sentinel*, 2 July 1876, as quoted in *Annals of Wyoming*, XLVIII (Spring 1976), p. 101.

5. Photograph furnished by Dr. Don Rickey Jr.

6. Hays City (Kansas) *Times*, 15 May 1886.

7. Tenor parts were commonly played on trombones.

8. Although the list in the Hays paper referred to 'tenor drum,' the photographs show it to be a snare drum.

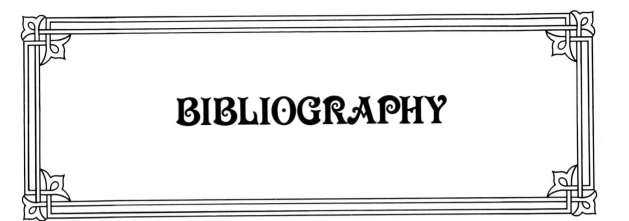

BIBLIOGRAPHY

PRIMARY SOURCES

A. MANUSCRIPTS

National Archives

Letters Received, Headquarters, Fort Hays, Kansas, Records of United States Army Commands, Record Group 393, National Archives and Records Service.

Letters Received, Office of the Quartermaster General, RG 92, NARS.

Letters Sent, Headquarters, Fort Hays, Kansas, RUSAC, RG 393, NARS.

Letters Sent, Headquarters, Fort Riley, Kansas, RUSAC, RG 393, NARS.

Letters Sent, Headquarters, Presidio of San Francisco, California, RUSAC, RG 393, NARS.

Letters Sent, Headquarters, Smoky Hill Subdistrict, RUSAC, RG 393, NARS.

Letters Sent, Office of the Quartermaster General, RG 92, NARS.

Post Orders, Headquarters, Fort Hays, Kansas, RUSAC, RG 393, NARS.

Post Returns, Fort Hays, Kansas, Adjutant General's Office, RG 94, NARS.

Post Returns, Fort Riley, Kansas, AGO, RG 94, NARS.

US Army, 6th Cavalry, Organizational Returns, AGO, RG 94, NARS.

State Archives

US Army, 7th Cavalry, Band and Noncommissioned Staff Order Book, 1890–91, Kansas State Historical Society.

Private Archives

George Crook Papers, United States Army Military History Research Collection, Carlisle Barracks, Pennsylvania.

Diary of Hartford G. Clark, Private, 6th Cavalry, Fort Niobrara, Nebraska, October–December 1891. Typescript copy furnished to authors by Dr Don Rickey Jr.

Letters of Robert Greenhalgh, Private, 2nd Cavalry, 1865–66. Typescript copy furnished to authors by Dr Don Rickey Jr.

B. PRINTED SOURCES

Published Official Documents

Annual Report of the Secretary of War, 1866–1900. Washington, US Government Printing Office, 1866–1900.

Budington, M. I., (ed.). *Uniform of the United States Army, 1774–1889.* Washington: The Quartermaster General, 1889.

Regulations for the Army of the United States, 1895. Washington: Government Printing Office, 1895.

US *Congressional Globe, Containing the Debates and Proceedings, 1833–1873.* 190 vols. Washington: Blair, Rives, *et al*, editors and publishers, 1834–1873.

US Congress, House. *Regimental Bands.* 37th Cong., 2nd sess., 1862, House Executive Document No. 72 (Serial 1134).

US Congress, House. *Revised Army Regulations.* 42nd Cong., 3rd sess., 1874, House Report No. 85, I (Serial 1576).

US Congress, House. Secretary of War, *Annual Report* (1875), House Executive Document No. 1, pt. II, 44th Cong., 2nd sess., I, 1876 (Serial 1674).

US Congress, House. *Regimental Bands for the Army.* 51st Cong., 1st sess., 1890, House Executive Document No. 446 (Serial 2752).

US War Department. *War of the Rebellion: A Compilation of Official Records of the Union and Confederate Armies.* 128 vols. Washington: Government Printing Office, 1880–1901.

Memoirs and Autobiographies

Baldwin, Alice Blackwood. *Memoirs of the Late Frank D. Baldwin Major General, USA.* Los Angeles, California: Wetzel Publishing Co., 1924.

Carrington, Frances C. *My Army Life.* Philadelphia: J. B. Lippincott, 1911.

Carrington, Margaret. *Absaraka: Home of the Crows.* Chicago: The Lakeside Press, 1950.

Custer, Elizabeth B. *Boots and Saddles: or Life in Dakota with General Custer.* Norman: University of Oklahoma Press, 1961.

Custer, Elizabeth B. *Following the Guidon.* Norman: University of Oklahoma Press, 1966.

Custer, George Armstrong. *My Life on the Plains.* Norman: University of Olkahoma Press, 1962.

Finerty, John J. *Warpath and Bivouac, or the Conquest of the Sioux.* Norman: University of Oklahoma Press, 1961.

Gibbon, John. *Gibbon on the Sioux Campaign of 1876.* Bellevue, Nebraska: The Old Army Press, 1969.

King, Captain Charles S. *Campaigning with Crook.* Norman: University of Oklahoma Press, 1964.

King, Captain Charles S. *The Colonel's Daughter or Winning His Spurs*. Philadelphia: J. B. Lippincott Co., 1895.

Roe, Frances M. A. *Army Letters from an Officer's Wife*. Lincoln: University of Nebraska Press, 1981.

Roland, Charles P. and Robbins, Richard, (eds.). 'The Diary of Eliza (Mrs. Albert Sidney) Johnston,' *Southwestern Historical Society Quarterly*, LX (April 1957)

Strong, General W. E. *A Trip to the Yellowstone National Park In July, August and September, 1875*. Norman: University of Oklahoma Press, 1968.

Summerhayes, Martha. *Vanished Arizona: Recollections of My Army Life*. Chicago: The Lakeside Press, 1939.

C. NEWSPAPERS

Ellis County *Free Press* (Hays, Kansas), 1885–1889.

Ellis County *Star* (Hays, Kansas), 1876–1882.

Hays City (Kansas) *Republican*, 1888–1889.

Hays City (Kansas) *Sentinel*, 1876–1889.

Hays City (Kansas) *Times*, 1886–1889.

Junction City (Kansas) *Union*, 4 April 1874.

The Rocky Mountain News (Denver, Colorado), 1888–1889.

St Louis *Daily Missouri Republican*, 10 December 1858.

Topeka (Kansas) *Commonwealth*, 2–6 July 1876.

D. BOOKS

Heitman, Francis B. (comp.). *Historical Register and Dictionary of the United States Army, 1789–1903*. 2 vols. Washington: Government Printing Office, 1903.

Knight, Oliver. *Life and Manners of the Frontier Army*. Norman: University of Oklahoma Press, 1978.

Price, George F. *Across the Continent with the Fifth Cavalry*. New York: Antiquarian Press, 1959.

Tucker, William Warren. *The Grand Duke Alexis in the United States of America*. New York: Interland Press, 1972.

Upton, Major General Emory. *Infantry Tactics, Double and Single Rank: Adapted to American Topography and Improved Firearms*. New York: Greenwood Press, 1968

E. OTHER

Dodworth, Allen. *Brass Band School*. New York: H. B. Dodworth and Co., 1853.

Friederich, G. W. E. *The Brass Band Journal*. New York: Firth, Pond and Co., 1853

Hine, Charles Delano. 'Uniform,' *The United Service: A Monthly Review of Military and Naval Affairs* (May 1895)

Letter, Franklin G. Smith, Superintendent: Chamizal National Memorial, El Paso, Texas, to author, 25 February 1974.

SECONDARY SOURCES

A. BOOKS

Athearn, Robert G. *William Tecumseh Sherman and the Settlement of the West*. Norman: University of Oklahoma Press, 1956.

Brown, Dee. *Fort Phil Kearney: An American Saga*. Lincoln: University of Nebraska Press, 1971.

Carpenter, Thomas J. and Fry, Rheda. *Old West Army Cookbook, 1865–1900*. Santa Fe: Museum of New Mexico, 1974.

Carriker, Robert. *Fort Supply, Indian Territory: Frontier Outpost on the Plains*. Norman: University of Oklahoma Press, 1970.

Cassin-Scott, Jack and Fabb, John. *Military Bands and their Uniforms*. Poole, Dorset, United Kingdom: Blandford Press, 1978.

Downey, Fairfax. *Fyfe, Drum & Bugle*. Fort Collins: The Old Army Press, 1971.

Elting, John R., (ed.). *Military Uniforms in America: The Era of the American Revolution, 1775–1795*. San Rafael, California: Presidio Press, 1974.

Elting, John R., (ed.). *Military Uniforms in America: Years of Growth, 1796–1851*. San Rafael, California: Presidio Press, 1977.

Foner, Jack D. *The United States Army Between Two Wars: Army Life and Reforms, 1865–1891*. New York: Humanities Press, 1970.

Fowler, Arlen W. *The Black Infantry in the West, 1865–1891*. Westport, Connecticut: Negro Universities Press, 1971.

Frink, Maurice, with Barthelmess, Casey. *Photographer on an Army Mule*. Norman: University of Oklahoma Press, 1965.

Frost, Lawrence. *The Court-Martial of General George Armstrong Custer*. Norman: University of Oklahoma Press, 1968.

Garofalo, Robert and Elrod, Mark. *A Pictorial History of Civil War Era Musical Instruments and Military Bands*. Charleston, West Virginia: Pictorial Histories Publishing Co., 1985.

Gray, John S. *Centennial Campaign*. Fort Collins: The Old Army Press, 1976.

Grinnell, George Bird. *Two Great Scouts and Their Pawnee Battalion*. Lincoln: University of Nebraska Press, 1973.

Hafen, LeRoy R., Hollon, W. Eugene, and Rister, Carl Coke. *Western America: The Exploration, Settlement, and Development of the Region Beyond the Mississippi*. Englewood Cliffs, New Jersey: Prentice and Hall, 1970.

Haley, James. *The Buffalo War*. New York: Doubleday and Co., 1976.

Higham, Robin and Brandt, Carol, (eds.). *The United States Army in Peacetime: Essays in Honor of the Bicentennial, 1775–1975*. Manhattan, Kansas: Military Affairs/Aerospace Historian Publishing, 1975.

Hoig, Stan. *The Battle of the Washita*. New York: Doubleday and Co., 1976.

Hoig, Stan. *The Sand Creek Massacre*. Norman: University of Oklahoma Press, 1961.

Hunt, Frazier, and Hunt, Robert. *I Fought with Custer: The Story of Sergeant Windolph*. New York: Charles Scribner's Sons, 1947.

Jackson, Donald. *Custer's Gold: The United States Cavalry Expedition of 1874*. Lincoln: University of Nebraska Press, 1972.

King, James T. *War Eagle: A Life of General Eugene A. Carr*. Lincoln: University of Nebraska Press, 1963.

Krause, Herbert and Olson, Gary D., (eds.). *Prelude to Glory: A Newspaper Accounting of Custer's 1874 Expedition to the Black Hills*. Sioux Falls, South Dakota: Brevet Press International, 1974.

Langellier, J. Phillip. *They Continually Wear the Blue: US Army Enlisted Dress Uniforms, 1865–1902*. San Francisco: Barnes-McGee, 1976.

Leckie, William H. *The Buffalo Soldiers: A Narrative of the Negro Cavalry in the West*. Norman: University of Oklahoma Press, 1967.

Lentz, Donald A. and Olsen, Walter R. *Gleanings from the First Century of Nebraska Bands, 1867–1967: Programs, Pictures and Some Recollections*. Lincoln: Word Services Publishing Co., 1979.

Lord, Francis A., and Wise, Arthur. *Bands and Drummer Boys of the Civil War*. New York: Thomas Yoseloff, 1966.

Todd, Frederick. *Soldiers of the American Army, 1775–1954*. Chicago: Henry Regnery Co., 1954.

Todd, Frederick, *et al. American Military Equipage, 1851–1872*. 3 vols. Providence, Rhode Island: The Company of Military Historians, 1974–76.

Utley, Robert M. *Frontier Regulars: The United States Army and the Indian, 1866–1891*. New York: Macmillan and Co., 1973.

Utley, Robert M. *Frontiersmen in Blue: The United States Army and the Indian, 1848–1865*. New York: Macmillan and Co., 1967.

Utley, Robert M. *The Last Days of the Sioux Nation*. New Haven: Yale University Press, 1963.

Utley, Robert M., (ed.). *Life in Custer's Cavalry: Diaries and Letters of Albert and Jennie Barnitz*. New Haven: Yale University Press, 1977.

Utley, Robert M., (ed.). *Soldier and Brave: Historic Places Associated with Indian Affairs and the Indian Wars in the Trans-Mississippi West*. Vol. XII of *The National Survey of Historic Sites and Buildings*. Edited by Robert G. Ferriss. Washington: Government Printing Office, 1971.

Vaughan, J. W. *The Reynolds Campaign on Powder River*. Norman: University of Oklahoma Press, 1966.

White, William Carter. *A History of Military Music in America*. New York: Greenwood Press, 1975.

Wiley, Bell I. *The Life of Billy Yank: The Common Soldier of the Union*. Garden City, New York: Doubleday and Co., 1971.

B. ARTICLES

Anderson, Simon V. 'The Unofficial Bands of the American Revolution,' *Music Educators Journal*, LXI (Dec. 1974), pp. 26–33.

Carroll, George P. 'The Band of Musick of the Second Virginia Regiment.' *Journal of Band Research*, II (No. 1), pp. 17–18.

Mattes, Merrill J. *Indians, Infants, and Infantry: Andrew and Elizabeth Burt on the Frontier*. Denver: Old West Publishing Co., 1960.

Merington, Marguerite, (ed.). *The Custer Story: The Life and Intimate Letters of General Custer and his wife Elizabeth*. New York: Devin-Adair, 1950.

Olson, James C. *Red Cloud and the Sioux Problem*. Lincoln: University of Nebraska Press, 1965.

Olson, Kenneth E. *Music and Musket: Bands and Bandsmen of the American Civil War*. Westport, Connecticut: Greenwood Press, 1981.

Priest, Loring B. *Uncle Sam's Stepchildren: The Reformation of United States Indian Policy, 1865–1887*. Lincoln: University of Nebraska Press, 1975.

Prucha, Francis Paul, S. J. *American Indian Policy in Crisis: Christian Reformers and the Indian, 1865–1900*. Norman: University of Oklahoma Press, 1976.

Prucha, Francis Paul, S. J. *Broadax and Bayonet: The Role of the United States Army in the Development of the Northwest, 1815–1860*. Lincoln: University of Nebraska Press, 1967.

Rickey, Don, Jr. *Forty Miles a Day on Beans and Hay: The Enlisted Soldier Fighting the Indian Wars*. Norman: University of Oklahoma Press, 1963.

Sonneck, Oscar. *Early Concert Life in America*. Wiesbaden, Germany: Dr. Martin Sandig, oHG, 1969.

Stewart, Edgar. *Custer's Luck*. Norman: University of Oklahoma Press, 1955.

Thrapp, Dan L. *The Conquest of Apacheria*. Norman: University of Oklahoma Press, 1967.

Carroll, John M. 'The Seventh Cavalry's Band,' *Little Big Horn Associates Research Review*, IX (Spring 1975), pp. 16–18.

Fitzpatrick, John C. 'The Bands of the Continental Army,' *Daughters of the American Revolution Magazine*, LVII (April 1923), pp. 187–97.

Gates, John P. 'The Alleged Isolation of US Army Officers in the Late 19th Century.' *Parameters*, X (Sep. 1980), pp. 32–45.

Railsback, Thomas C. 'Military Bands and Music at Old Fort Hays, 1867–1889,' *Journal of the West*, XX (July 1983), pp. 28–35.

C. THESES, DISSERTATIONS AND MANUSCRIPTS

Buchanan, John S. 'Functions of the Fort Davis Military Bands and Musical Proclivities of the Commanding Officer, Colonel Benjamin H. Grierson, Late Nineteenth Century.' Unpublished Master's thesis, Department of Music, Sul Ross State College, 1968.

Bufkin, William A. 'Union Bands of the Civil War (1862–1865): Instrumentation and Score Analysis.' Unpublished Doctoral dissertation, School of Music, Louisiana State University, 1973.

Camus, Raoul F. 'The Military Band in the United States Army Prior to 1834.' Unpublished Doctoral dissertation, School of Education, New York University, 1969.

Olson, Kenneth E. 'Yankee Bands of the Civil War.' Unpublished Doctoral dissertation, School of Music, University of Minnesota, 1971.

Patrick, Stewart G. 'A History of the Regimental Bands of Minnesota During the Civil War.' Unpublished Doctoral dissertation, School of Music, University of North Dakota, 1972.

Powell, Anthony L. 'Keep Step to the Music of the Union: A History of Black Regular Army Bands, 1869–1930.' Unpublished manuscript, San Jose, California, 1980.

Zwink, Timothy A. 'The Hancock-Custer Expedition of 1867.' Unpublished Master's thesis, Department of History, Fort Hays State University, 1974.

D. DISCOGRAPHY

Company of Military Historians. Military Music in America, Vol. III: *The Army in the West, 1870–1890*. Providence: Company of Military Historians, n.d.

Company of Military Historians. Military Music in America, Vol. IV: *The Union Army Band*. Providence: Company of Military Historians, 1969.

Eastman Wind Ensemble, Frederick Fennell, conductor. *Ruffles and Flourishes*. Rochester: Eastman School of Music, n.d. Mercury Records SRI 78034.

Eastman Wind Ensemble, Frederick Fennell, conductor. *Music of the Civil War*. Rochester: Eastman School of Music, n.d. Mercury Records SRI 2–77011.

Eastman Wind Ensemble, Frederick Fennell, conductor. *The Spirit of '76*. Rochester: Eastman School of Music, n.d. Mercury Records SRI 75048.

Eastman Wind Ensemble, Donald Hunsberger, conductor. *Homespun America*. Rochester: Eastman School of Music, 1976. Vox Productions, Inc., SVBX 5309.

Empire Brass Quintet. *The American Brass Band Journal*. Boston: Empire Brass Quintet. Columbia Records M 34192.